PRAISE FOR

Susan Pohlman takes us on a journey of the soul down Italy's cobblestone streets and through magnificent cathedrals in search of life's meaning at midlife. This is an exquisite book that urges us to look up and look inward with eyes open to the grace around us. With lyrical prose and vulnerability, Pohlman leads us quietly to a spiritual awakening.

— Teri Rizvi, founder and director, Erma Bombeck Writers' Workshop

"For all of those poised on the edge of the empty nest, Susan Pohlman's new memoir is a must-read. *A Time to Seek* grabs the heart and doesn't let go."

—Lee Woodruff, speaker and best-selling author of *In an Instant, Perfectly Imperfect - A Life in Progress*, and *Those We Love Most.*

In *A Time to Seek*, Susan Pohlman's rich, warm and spiritual meditation on midlife, she writes, "The longer you travel, the more you turn into yourself." Yes, indeed. *A Time to Seek* is filled with memorable moments and spot-on observations about creating a new sense of self, connecting to a higher power and making the most of your years. Plus, arm-chair traveling of the highest order! What an adventure she takes us on, as she returns to Florence, Genoa and Rome in search of peace and purpose. Laughter, learning and plenty of gelato. Highly Recommend.

— Lian Dolan, producer and host of *Satellite Sisters,* and author of two Los Angeles Times best-selling novels, *Helen of Pasadena* and *Elizabeth the First Wife,* and soon to be published *The Sweeney Sisters.*

With her trademark warmth and inspiration, Susan Pohlman has penned a lyrical journey of personal transformation. She delivers an essential tale, rich with the unquenchable yearning of midlife transition. This book asks you to revisit the person you were before the world told you who to be, taking you on one woman's nostalgic adventure of discovery.

—Windy Lynn Harris, author of *Writing & Selling Short Stories & Personal Essays: The Essential Guide to Getting Your Work Published*

"With wisdom, reverence, and grace, Susan Pohlman delivers a lyrical meditation on midlife and mother-hood while traveling the cobblestoned streets of Florence, Genoa, and Rome. *A Time to Seek* is an absolute gem for those navigating the empty nest or a period of personal transition. I loved this book! " — Laura Munson, *New York Times* best-selling author and founder of the acclaimed Haven Writing Retreats.

"It takes a special kind of courage and willingness to be honest in midlife. Susan Pohlman, in *A Time to Seek*, artfully considers the intersection between motherhood, travel, and the reshaping of her personal narrative. Pohlman pulls the reader into a journey that's honest and redemptive, spontaneous and contemplative, and ultimately, a way to cultivate faith when confronting hard truths. Readers will find Pohlman's voice comforting and relatable — and perhaps a good reminder to question and probe even when it isn't convenient.

—Rudri Bhatt Patel, Founder and Editor of *The Sunlight Press*

"Navigating the dicey road into her fifth decade, Susan Pohlman takes us on her inner journey in search of answers as she begins to release her identity as "Mom." Traversing the beauty of both her own heart and the intrinsic beauty of Italy, we witness the fullness of her next becoming in her vulnerable and poetic prose."

~Arielle Ford, author of *Turn Your Mate Into Your Soulmate*

Susan's second book had me hooked right from the beginning. As a wife and mother staring middle-age and the empty nest right in the eye, I continually rooted for the author throughout her series of Italian adventures while simultaneously reflecting on my own life.

—Amy Carney, author of *Parent on Purpose: A Courageous Approach to Raising Children in a Complicated World*

Life's steady pull to the next moment, rarely suggests a long, deep breath, a meaningful pause. With great intention, we must make it otherwise. We must see what awaits when we seek a deeper truth. Open *A Time to Seek*, a book with a timeless message and universal purpose, and journey forth with this experienced traveler, this insightful author. It's the perfect antidote for troubled times. Clarity and mystery, endings and beginnings, merge beautifully in this wondrous new memoir by Susan Pohlman; it will hold you spellbound.

--D. A. Hickman, author of *A Happy Truth, The Silence of Morning,* and *Ancients of the Earth: Poems of Time.*

A Time to Seek is a brave, heartfelt, beautifully written exploration of the journey into midlife. Susan Pohlman uses the transformative power of travel to delve deep into her own sense of identity, spirituality, faith, love, and family. Enlightening and engaging reading, this book is a must-read for anyone struggling to confront change with grace and wisdom.

—Karen McCann, author of *Dancing in the Fountain: How to Enjoy Living Abroad*

A TIME TO SEEK

MEANING, PURPOSE, AND SPIRITUALITY AT MIDLIFE

SUSAN POHLMAN

A Time to Seek

Published by Riviera Publishing

Copyright © 2020 by Susan Pohlman

978-1-7346132-3-0 (Print)

978-1-7346132-2-3 (eBook)

Cover: Katie Bussoletti

For my mother

For everything there is a season, and a time for
every matter under heaven:
a time to be born, and a time to die;
a time to plant, and a time to pluck up what is
planted;
a time to kill, and a time to heal;
a time to break down, and a time to build up;
a time to weep, and a time to laugh;
a time to mourn, and a time to dance;
a time to cast away stones,
and a time to gather stones together;
a time to embrace, and a time to refrain from
embracing;
a time to seek, and a time to lose;
a time to keep, and a time to cast away;
a time to tear, and a time to sew;
a time to keep silence, and a time to speak;
a time to love, and a time to hate;
a time for war, and a time for peace.
—Ecclesiastes 3:1–8 (ESV)

PROLOGUE

It sneaked up on me—a few extra pounds, an unflattering reflection in a store window, a teen who called me "ma'am" and offered me his seat on the bus. One day I looked around, and it dawned on me that *other* people were seeing me differently.

It was not my best day.

Midlife begins quietly; there is no celebratory rite of passage or ritual to mark its onset. Our culture does not greet it with high-fives or open arms or recognition for a half century well done. Instead we receive birthday cards that tell us we are over the hill. So, we do our best to deny our aging for as long as possible which only prolongs our ability to make peace with it.

We are often left to figure out this complicated transition by ourselves. For many of us, it can be a lonely and confusing time as long buried or newfound yearnings claw their way into our consciousness, often disturbing carefully constructed lives. We turn to books and medical professionals for information; friends, husbands, and significant others for comfort; the privacy of a personal journal to make sense of our changing bodies and evolving roles. And we pray a lot.

Transition, however, doesn't have to be dark and scary. It doesn't have to be a crisis. It can be interesting, exciting, and rejuvenating—a time of renewal. I have learned to recognize the unquenchable yearnings and wobbly footing during midlife for what they are: actual graces. Divine nudges. God calling us to a deeper understanding of ourselves and the many purposes of our lives. Whether we are ready or not, we enter new phases of life as we age and, sometimes, we need to gift ourselves with time to ponder life's great questions in order to find clarity to move forward in a meaningful way though our next chapter. At this time of our lives, God calls us to seek.

This recognition of unquenchable yearning as the call to spiritual growth did not come cheaply. It took great sacrifice and personal upheaval for me to let go of the life I had carefully constructed so that God could teach me how to seek him in a way that I could hear him. In 2003, as told in *Halfway to Each Other: How a Year in Italy Brought our Family Home*, my husband and I made an improbable decision to sign a lease to an apartment overlooking the sea near Genoa, Italy, rather than divorce papers. We sold our home, quit our jobs, and moved there with our two stunned children, ages eleven and fourteen, hoping to find our way back to each other. Our deep yearning to save our family propelled us past conventional thinking and taught us a thing or two about God's mighty love and mysterious ways. It taught us that grace changes everything.

When I found myself restless and unsettled as I turned fifty, I decided to again use travel to work through the transitional themes of grief, surrender, love, faith, letting go, and acceptance. Travel is a magical way to seek, and adventure is a powerful and compelling teacher. The outer journey stimulates the inner journey. When we slip out of our cultural constraints and experience our great world in new ways, we find ourselves opening to possibility, imagining a life of greater meaning, and seeing our lives from a new perspective. When we travel with prayerful intention, we discover things about ourselves that might otherwise continue to lie hidden. The varying landscapes, the people we meet along the way, and the flavors and textures we find before us are riddled with lessons. God speaks to the soul in serendipitous moments.

Whether defined by a weekend at the beach or a trip around the world, travel grants us much needed emotional breathing room to pray and listen; it grants us space to address our spiritual needs. It is my hope that by sharing these experiences with you that you might set off on a pilgrimage of your own.

This book was inspired by a journey that I took to Italy with my daughter, Katie. The trip was an unexpected gift from my husband to help her get settled into a semester abroad program.

When I landed in Italy, I let go of all preconceived notions about midlife and motherhood and prayed for the divine to inspire and enlighten me on this pilgrimage of sorts—to lead me to a deeper sense of myself in this stage of life.

I invite you to pack your bags and journey with me~

CHAPTER 1

A Time to Seek

Sacred journeys are the ones we remember all of our lives. They often occur during times when we find ourselves at a crossroads, plagued with a longing or yearning that we don't fully understand. They are about more than sightseeing, more than artwork or ancient ruins or exotic landscapes. Something deep within calls us forward and inward, giving us a sense that something holy is unfolding, and it is important to pay attention. Choosing to follow this "calling forth" is choosing to gift ourselves with time away from social constraints and cultural clutter—time for self-reflection to assess how and why our lives may be changing—what chapters might be coming to an end, and what new ones may be beginning. Sacred journeys don't necessarily change our lives, but they help us change the way we see life. And there is often great peace in that turn of the lens.

This particular journey was a gift. Looking back, I see that it came straight from heaven. And how appropriate that it arrived on Christmas Day.

Six of us were in the family room that morning vying for position around a twinkling Christmas tree. Candles flickered along a pine-strewn mantle, and a roaring fire gave the room an orange glow, a welcome addition to the (rare!) rainy Arizona morning. A jazzy rendition of "Winter Wonderland" lifted my spirits as I topped off my parents' coffee cups and threw the first of many holiday treats to our dogs, Zucca and Caramel.

I was sensing the passing of time this season. There was an unexplained ache in my heart that I kept shooing away. Maybe it was my looming benchmark birthday, but I interpreted every unspoken nuance as a sign of getting older. My dad now leaned on a blue metallic cane. Tim, my husband of twenty-four years, tromped around in slippers with broken-down heels. And my mom wore a teal velour running suit, though I couldn't remember the last time I had seen her run. This would be the final Christmas of my forties, and I wanted the day to last forever. I was, for the first time, fearful of the forward movement of the seasons. I was afraid because important things in my life were starting to end.

Two weeks before, I had decorated the house for the holidays. Alone. I wept the whole way through. For two decades Decorating Night had always been a family frenzy. Pulling out the boxes, blowing the dust off of ornaments and memories, placing the brass reindeer, lighting candles. Funny fights over who would unpack the manger and who would arrange the mantel. This year, though, it was quiet and orderly. I opened one box at a time and put everything in its place. Since when would that lead to a Christmasy feeling?

This year was about logistics, about a father and son at a volleyball tournament in Anaheim and a daughter at college in San Francisco. Who can't fit in a few hours of placing memories on kitchen counters and windowsills? A family moving on, that's who.

"Come on, Mom. Hurry," implored Matthew, my seventeen-year-old, who had grown into a mannish conglomeration when I wasn't looking. At six feet, eight inches tall, he was a tangle of legs and arms, but he continued to poke through the mound of gifts like a seven-year-old.

"Will says hello," Katie, twenty-one, yelled from the couch as she piled her blonde hair into a sloppy knot with one hand and scrolled through a text message from her boyfriend with the other. "His parents gave him a Eurail pass for Christmas. Isn't that great?" She and Will were gearing up for a semester abroad in Florence. They were leaving in a few weeks, and Katie was a bundle of nerves, barely able to talk about anything else.

"Does everyone have their Santa caps?" Tim asked as he held up a red felt triangle and smiled in my direction. Pulling it on his head, his blue eyes twinkled beneath a narrow strip of fake fur, feathered and gray from two decades of Christmas mornings. I loved how much he loved this day. We shared a knowing smile, and I put my cap on, checking my reflection in the oven door.

Heavy drops of rain drummed against the window like impatient fingertips. I pulled my white robe around me and, with steaming coffee in hand, wiggled onto the couch between Katie and my mother, the three of us instinctually leaning into each other, preparing to exchange holy sarcasm when necessary. We were finally ready to begin the long-awaited *Opening of the Gifts Ceremony.*

Unlike the chaos I remembered from growing up with five brothers—tearing into our boxes at warp speed, wrapping paper exploding into shreds—we had adopted Tim's family tradition, one that we all now revered. Matthew had assumed Tim's former childhood role as the Passer-Outer of Presents. With pinkies arched upward, he would ceremoniously don his Santa cap, nod to all, and then slowly work his way through the boxes and gift bags, making sure that everyone got a chance to open them in a fair and measured fashion.

The usual order of events went as follows:

1. Selection of a gift after a fake prolonged search
2. Presentation to the recipient, who opens it slowly to add to the suspense
3. Handing all reusable ribbon and gift bags over to me
4. Dramatic display of the gift, with much gawking and admiring from the recipient
5. Oohs and aahs from all
6. Flurry of "Thank yous" and "Don't mention its"
7. Deafening round of applause
8. Repeat

Including coffee and bathroom breaks, opening Christmas gifts at our house generally lasts over two hours, and we love every dragged-out minute of it. About three-quarters through the ceremony that morning, Tim directed Matthew toward an ordinary envelope propped against the cinnamon-colored wall behind the tree.

"Give that to your mother," he said as an anxious look clouded his face. Since we had already splurged on new bedroom furniture as our mutual Christmas gift, I was surprised.

Smiling, I took it from Matthew. Unmarked envelopes were a good sign, usually holding a gift certificate. I turned the envelope over, smooth and white in my hand, lifted the flap, and took out a sheet of printer paper folded like a business letter.

"What does it say?" Katie asked, leaning over my shoulder to catch a glimpse.

"Give me a second," I said as I unfolded the note. On it was something so unexpected that I sat stunned, mouth agape and eyes tearing, unable to perform step four—the requisite dramatic display of the gift. All I could muster was to hold up, with shaking hands, the piece of paper with its one sentence in red-and-green oversized font:

Week in Florence with Katie . . . January 26th . . . Get packing!

Everyone screamed. I looked across the room at Tim, whose eyes were tearing up faster than mine, and I ran to give him the biggest hug of my life. He was sending me to Florence? "What on earth?" I asked.

"Go have fun," Tim said. "You can help Katie get settled."

"We can't afford. . ."

"Airline miles. Don't worry." He grinned, waving my concern away with the flick of his wrist.

As step number seven—the deafening round of applause—came to a close, I caught Katie's eye. In an instant, I knew that the big smile pasted across her face was about as genuine as that of a first runner-up in a beauty pageant. Though she didn't want to hurt my feelings, it was clear she wasn't sure how to take this unlikely turn of events, and I could hardly blame her. I gave her a quick eyebrow raise, and she nodded, knowing we would discuss it by ourselves another time. I would assure her that I would remain invisible and not cramp her style.

The room soon calmed, and the gift-opening ceremony continued. Matthew next chose a silver-wrapped box and handed it to my mother, who began her yearly speech about how she didn't need gifts and how just being there was her gift. As she fiddled with the ribbon, I took a deep breath and closed my eyes, returning for a moment to Italy. I remembered worn cobblestones beneath my feet, the musty scent of churches, and the artwork of the masters that had awoken a powerful yearning in my soul. I could almost hear the musicality of the Italian language and taste the ruby wine, lush and earthy.

At the lowest emotional point of my life, Florence had saved me, helped restore meaning to my days. It was there that I began to listen to my own heart and take myself seriously. For me, Florence became an avenue toward transcendence and enlightenment, toward a renaissance of my own. It was where I had dared to trust God, wholly. In so doing, I learned great lessons about the power of surrender: how mighty it could be; how it opened my soul. Where I learned to be present in every moment and open my eyes to God's graces all around me.

Explaining that I needed to cut the coffee cake, I stood and headed for the kitchen as my mother admired new slippers. But the truth was that I was overwhelmed with a rush of emotion. As I waded through a pile of mangled wrapping paper and curls of ribbon, I realized, in a flash that took my breath away, that, perhaps, I was being *called* back to Italy. The room swirled, and I grabbed the counter to steady myself. I had been through this before, and I knew that once you realize you have been called, there is no escape.

As the room stopped spinning I felt immense relief rather than the paralyzing fear I had felt the first time I said yes to Italy. Midlife was knocking at the door and I had recently noticed myself becoming unhinged. I had fallen back into some of my old traps and routines, and I had been struggling with a spiritual emptiness that my parish priest assured me was a normal ebb and flow of life. I needed to turn toward God. I needed to seek him.

As I opened the refrigerator to grab a fruit plate, I glanced into the family room, my eyes resting on our little manger scene on the mantel. It had been a wedding gift that had traveled with us through twenty-five Christmases. Our tradition was to place the baby Jesus in the manger before opening presents and saying a prayer of gratitude for our many blessings. My heart sank as I saw that the manger, today, was empty. How telling that we had all forgotten to begin there.

CHAPTER 2

Like a Shooting Star

I listened to Tim's slow and measured breathing and felt the comforting weight of him sleeping next to me. Zucca, a thicket of curly, black poodle hair, was nestled snug against my leg. A nightmare had inserted itself into a perfectly fine sleep and ruined it, forcing me to lie awake in the dark and think. As middle of the nights go, this was standard fare. Insomnia would follow, providing me with time to continue chewing on the obsession of the moment.

Now wide-awake, I slung my legs over the side of the bed and stood, my toes burrowing into the beige carpet. I wandered into the darkened living room, my nightgown the gray white of a restive ghost. I paused before the front hall mirror, the one that used to hang in the entryway of my childhood home. This mirror had watched me grow up. Helped me button coats and tie scarves against the New Jersey winters, warned me of misplaced strands of hair before I opened the door to my first date, and witnessed my last deep breath as I set out for the church on my wedding day. Lately, I found myself avoiding it. I did not want it to see me grow old.

Tonight, though, I looked straight into my own eyes, and instead of scrutinizing my melting features, I was drawn to the reflection of our backyard pool through the glass windows along the living room wall behind me. The surface of the water caught the moonlight in slivers. I grabbed a thick holiday blanket off of the couch and wrapped it around me as I tiptoed through the kitchen. The tiny white lights were still twinkling on the tree in the family room, and our piles of opened gifts were strewn haphazardly around the room. I have always loved the happy mayhem of Christmas night.

I pushed aside some books and a fawn-colored turtleneck and grabbed Tim's gift envelope with its single sheet inside, now worn from over-reading. I slid the patio door open and slipped into the Arizona night. The icy breath off the desert was just enough to stir the palm trees and oleander, their rustling leaves like the whispers of teenage girls.

The flagstone, pallid in the light of the moon, was smooth and cold against my bare feet as I walked to a chaise lounge that sat next to the pool. I lay down, positioned the blanket around me, and relaxed. Clutching the letter to my chest, I breathed in a silence so absolute that I imagined I was the only soul awake for miles. I felt the negative energy from my unquiet heart dissipate as I looked upward through the fronds of the palm trees to a glittering sky.

I was still in shock about my extremely wonderful gift. The perfectness of it. Tim knew that Katie was a bit wobbly about going back overseas, as her track record with transition wasn't great. She'd be fine once she settled into her new surroundings but getting there would be like an arrow shot through a windstorm that somehow hits the bull's-eye. Getting there would take some support.

What Tim did not know was that this trip was an answer to my prayers. Lately, I couldn't shake the feeling that my life also resembled that arrow being tussled about in the windstorm. For me, however, there was no target in sight. We were now, unexpectedly, settled into a life in Scottsdale (moving into our thirteenth house since we had gotten married). Tim had started a business that began with a flourish, and we'd bought a home. Approximately five minutes later, the 2007 recession began in earnest. Would the business make it? Would our house lose its value? Would we end up selling our couches on the curb? I had an extremely bad feeling about the whole situation.

Then, this past July, during the interview process for

a coveted administrative position at a nearby school, I suffered the loss of my uterus in a surprise-attack hysterectomy, the timing of which ejected me from the pool of candidates. I was heartbroken, as such job openings were rare, and I needed one. The recession was gaining momentum, and we needed stability in case things didn't go as planned. The writing life was great, but I was quickly learning that only a small percentage of writers can earn a decent living with their craft.

My ob-gyn had looked me straight in the eye after my yearly exam and said matter-of-factly, "Are you aware that your uterus is falling out?"

"Now that you mention it, I have felt some pressure," I said, looking down at my stomach.

"You should have come in sooner. You have a serious situation here," she murmured as she wrote something on her clipboard. I imagined she was drawing a stick figure of me with an arrow to the word *idiot*.

To make matters worse, my moods boarded a roller coaster and rode with abandon. I found myself crying when laughter would have been appropriate and giggling at critical moments that demanded reverent silence. My sentiments were all jumbled. My inappropriate weepiness became a running family joke—their favorite was the day I cried at a particularly tender scene in *The Incredibles*, a Pixar animated movie about washed-up superheroes. That landed me back in the doctor's office, and I left with testosterone cream and an estrogen patch that I was instructed to paste to my groin every three days.

A gust of wind sent a shiver through me, so I pulled the blanket under my chin and around my ears. Taking long, slow breaths, I filled my lungs with the cold air, the wind now blowing around me and through me at the same time. Becoming part of the night rather than the intruder, I rested for a few moments in my wool cocoon and relaxed into a hopeful peacefulness. Shreds of clouds floated across a three-quarter moon, and a lone coyote yelped in the distance.

My midlife disequilibrium began unexpectedly. I started experiencing pseudo panic attacks when Katie left for college, a feeling that I couldn't inhale deeply enough. The doctor assured me that it was nothing major—this was life. Katie was happy and thriving on her campus in California, but I missed her desperately. Even when we think we are ready to send our kids off to college, it's hard to see an empty bedroom.

And I was jealous.

It took me a while to own that feeling. What kind of mother admits that part of the angst of dropping my daughter off at school was the sudden realization that I wanted to be her? I wanted to be starting again. I had forgotten about the raw sexual energy of a college campus, the excitement of higher learning, the intoxication of questioning. I wanted to be free to roam, free to learn. I wanted to be able to want. Of course, all of this wanting was ridiculous. I loved my family, and I didn't *really* want to *go* anywhere, but my spirit began to rattle its cage.

I awoke one Wednesday and observed myself in the mirror as I applied my new special cream and affixed my new estrogen patch. Who was this restless woman standing here minus a uterus and sporting fake hormones? It scared me. I knew what came next—skin tags and hair loss. That panicky feeling returned, and I gulped for air. Why was I putting so much pressure on myself all of a sudden?

I had two more years until Matthew would leave for college. I loved having him home alone with us—giving us time to enjoy him front and center, but I was already fearful of the upcoming empty house. Already fearful of an empty me. My children were not just graduating from high school; *they were graduating from us.* You would think that I'd be an expert in navigating change since we had moved so many times, but this was different. I was always the same person during those moves, playing the same role. I was the mom doing "mom things." I didn't have recent experience in doing things that weren't mom-ish. Who was I to become now that I had no children at home to blame my constraints and failures on? I honestly did not have the energy for redefinition. The whole idea was disturbing, so I handled those thoughts like I always did, by quashing them, throwing in a few loads of laundry, and heading to do some errands.

I spent many an evening with a bowl of denial in one hand and a glass of wine in the other. I filled my journal with essays about time. One night it would be a poetic discourse about how its passing was marked by sunlight, moonlight, and starlight. Then the next, an angry attack about how I resented its subtly imprinting itself on my body and etching its memory into my face. How it ruled the world and how it imprisoned it. How I loved it, and how I feared it. How it continued to march me, like a clingy, school phobic child, down corridors I was not ready to walk.

I began reading articles and books about midlife. There were dramatic stories of crisis, reinvention, and anger sometimes aimed at entire generations of societal philosophy. Tales of women who handled this transition by narrowing their scope to what they could control. *Plant a garden! Feed the children in Burma!* Others took off for the unknown and never came back, discarding husbands and careers willy-nilly.

A few of the readings were thought-provoking and poignant, and I especially appreciated revisiting basic research in human psychology that I hadn't referred to since college. I refreshed my understanding of my id, ego, and superego, and contemplated Abraham Maslow's take on self-actualization. I agreed with Erich Fromm's needs for stimulation, unity, and effectiveness. I pored over Erik Erikson's ideas on generativity and integrity and nodded in agreement as I reread Carl

Rogers's definition of what it means to be a fully functioning person.

Regardless of the psychological school of thought, it was apparent that most of these experts agreed that there was enough going on socially and emotionally that this life stage deserved its own designation. There was an underlying awareness that at this tender time we are searching for meaning, authenticity, and a redefining of our relationship with and contribution to the universe. We want reassurance that our life choices have been worth the ride, and, if not, that it's not too late to change.

After all the reading, I reluctantly embraced the fact that I was in the midst of a profound and personal transition. Like all transitions, it would probably prove to be rocky. I was grieving on many levels. My autumn had begun, and I had not prepared for the change of season. I was a tall, spreading maple not ready to lose my leaves and, yet, I could sense an excitement at the hint of color that was seeping through my branches— scarlets and golds, and an orange that matched the sunrise.

Though I understood I was entering transition, it didn't mean that I knew the answers to my questions, the greatest of which was why I was so antsy and agitated when my life had seemed perfectly fine just six months ago. Perhaps I was being silly and only riding the thrill of possibility, like a huge swell in the ocean that lifts your toes from the sand and delights you with a sense of freedom and weightlessness before delivering you back to the safety of two feet planted ashore.

Suppressed restlessness became a pebble in my shoe. I sensed an overpowering need to travel again. Travel was my salve. I understood, as a result of my time abroad, its regenerative nature. I needed to go somewhere far away and ponder myself through this transformation, into a deeper understanding of myself. But let's face it—travel is expensive. This was not something you casually mention to your husband after a long day at work when a recession is starting. *Honey, I'm having a hard time hearing the language of my heart. Have you noticed that I'm starting to lose my identity? Have you seen it anywhere? I think it might be in Europe.*

Instead of sharing my predictable, boring, self-absorbed midlife angst with Tim, I began without realizing it, to study the expansive Arizona sky. I was inexplicably drawn to it, more than usual. For some primal reason I had yet to figure out, I needed to look upward. I would assess the exact shade of blue at noon, drink in the cascading hues that drenched the heavens at sunset and sneak out to the patio for a peek after dark while Tim and Matthew watched sports.

The evenings were particularly satisfying. Every night was a new show: the moon danced, and the clouds rearranged themselves in a myriad of combinations. There was the added element of the mystery of the deep black heavens, the vastness of creation, and the complexities of a universe I had no hopes of understanding. The night held an intimacy; it made me feel small and manageable. And the stars—well, I have a thing about stars. They are the celebrities of heaven. Charismatic and reliable, even one can charm a stormy sky.

Laying here now under this Christmas night sky sensing God's infinite majesty, I realized with a burning shame that what I did *not* do through all of this angst was pray for grace. I did not pray for knowledge and understanding. I did not pray for wisdom or fortitude. I was so sidelined by fear and grief, so undone by my changing body and emotional confusion that I couldn't see beyond them. I had let earthly, though deeply human, concerns paralyze me, close me to a godly perspective of life and the numerous gifts that have been bestowed upon me and my family.

It was no wonder that I had been mired in a period of spiritual emptiness. I needed, once more, to step out of this self-absorption, detach myself from the material and fill myself with the spiritual. Like a little girl reaching up to take my father's hand I needed, again, to let myself be led.

If I could, I would take the white envelope that contained my extremely wonderful gift and pin it to the sky. I could feel the magic of this upcoming adventure, see its shimmer. It would become my great star in the east, and I would follow its promise with the open heart of one of the Three Kings, not knowing the riches I would kneel before. I would come to understand this transition into my fifties by letting go and letting the Lord guide me. The wisdom I needed to navigate the next chapter of life might come to me if I was ready to let myself become vulnerable.

A golden arc streaked overhead, and my soul reached for it—a shooting star, brilliant in its final assignment. Beyond glorious to witness, it was a bonus for breaking the rules of sleep in a suburban neighborhood.

At that moment, lying on that chaise lounge swaddled in a Santa Claus blanket, I decided to take this decade and turn it on its ear. I promised myself to become a woman who sees insomnia as an opportunity for unexpected blessings. To recognize that this gift of adventure was the chance to begin my journey as a shooting star. To actively embrace life like the plain old ever-circling meteoroid who accepts the invitation to the ball, puts on a sequined gown, and becomes the meteor that dances across a cobalt sky and into the hearts of those lucky enough to notice. I would begin to figure out how to do this in Florence. I would clarify what was making me anxious and chart a new course that would, hopefully, replace feelings of anxiety and fear with purpose and contentment.

Exhilarated and peaceful, I climbed off the chaise lounge, padded across the pallid flagstone, and expertly slid the door open without so much as a squeak. I kissed the white envelope, wrinkled from a recent clutching to the heart, and laid it beside the fawn-colored turtleneck. I tiptoed across the cool tile, past the mirror edged in gold, and onto the beige carpet, and slipped ever so gently back under the covers. My dog nuzzled against my leg, and Tim's measured breathing assured me that all was fine, for now.

CHAPTER 3

A Time for Every Purpose

I chopped scallions as Katie circled the kitchen in faded jeans and a zipper-front, red sweatshirt. I knew this routine. It would go on for a few minutes while she sifted through the words tumbling in her brain. She grabbed a glass from the cabinet and filled it with water, opened the fridge, and stared into it. Closed it. Opened it again while gulping some water. Closed it. Looked through the junk drawer for something she didn't need. Finally, she stopped and stared me square in the face, eyes narrowed.

"I don't need someone to help me. I can do it myself." How many times had I heard that in the last twenty years?

"Of course, you can." I started on the celery.

"It's embarrassing," she said. "Dad didn't even ask me if it was okay."

"I won't be on the same flight."

"Oh, I'm supposed to pretend that my mother just happened to be in Florence the same week I start school? I can see it now, 'Hey, new roommates, look! There goes my mother, of all people. What's she doing here?'"

I handed her a paring knife and pointed to the tomatoes. She began slicing. I washed and peeled a few carrots. Katie and I stood side by side and chopped vegetables for a few quiet moments. The grind and thump of steel against wood carving boards had been the background music of many conversations over the years. Funny how it was easier to talk when our hands are busy.

Katie had spent the four years since our time in Liguria with one foot in each culture. Her transition back to the states had not been a smooth one, though she did eventually settle back into the flow of America. She had clung to her love of Italy by choosing to minor in Italian at college, and this semester in Florence was a long-held dream come true. However, the reality of moving across the ocean again was stirring all sorts of anxious memories. The reality of something rarely looks like the dream.

Though I was looking forward to this trip, I was having the usual second thoughts. Does it cost too much? Is this a good time? What if Matthew needs help with school? What if Katie holds this against me? Who will walk the dog? Cook dinner? Make sure the doors are locked at night?

Maybe I shouldn't go.

We can't afford it. I'm too old, too young, too fat, too skinny. I'm not worthy. Tim should go. We should go together. My parents need me. I have terrible hair for travel. I still don't understand foreign electrical currents.

Maybe I shouldn't go.

For years, I had talked myself out of solo travel opportunities with creative and elaborate reasoning. My parenting instincts overruled the desire to indulge in such craziness. But then I realized that the real craziness was assuming that my family could not fend for themselves for a week, and assuming that I didn't need these soul journeys to expand my sense of self to stay centered and emotionally and spiritually strong. We need to take the time for this purpose.

One of the truths that I took home with me after my expat year in Italy was a deepening awareness of our basic human instinct for adventure. Since the beginning of time, courageous men and women have answered that quietly persistent call to seek the unknown, embrace the uncomfortable, explore the edges of the civilized world. They were the ones to discover new lands, new philosophies, and greater expanses of universe. They changed the world, defined eras, self-actualized.

God designed us to seek. At our core is a constant emotional and spiritual desire for something more, something bigger. Unfortunately, our structured and sedentary lifestyles do not readily allow the wiggle room for adventure, yet it is what keeps us feeling vital and energized and close to the divine.

I decided to lower the volume on the random stream of consciousness that had been hounding me with lists of reasons not to go on this trip. I recognized the source of this reasoning for what it was: fear. Not a good reason for me to turn a deaf ear to grace. Besides, taking risks makes me feel like I am living my life and not just watching it from the bleachers.

"Katie, Dad already bought the ticket. He made this decision from a place of love. It's done. I'll travel alone; I won't embarrass you. Florence is a big place." Katie's eyes bored holes into mine. Though she was trying to be brave, a mother can see beyond a defiant stare. "I'll spend a few of the days in Genoa as well. Before you know it, I'll be gone," I added. "Besides, I may be too busy to even fit you in."

Katie reached for the last carrot, which she chopped as loudly as humanly possible. When she finished, I scooped the orange chunks into the salad bowl and chuckled. "I've never felt sorry for a carrot before." As we looked at each other over the cutting board, she took a deep breath, and a twinkle of acceptance came to her eyes.

"It does sort of help, knowing you'll be in the same

city if I need anything to start. We could probably go to dinner a few times. I guess it'll be fine. It's not how I pictured it—that's all."

"I know."

"I already told Will and Laura anyway," she admitted. "I said you were coming to Italy because of your first book. I had to think of something."

"What did they say?"

"It makes them feel more comfortable."

"Well, there you have it."

Matthew loped into the room, sprang upward, and touched the ceiling, just because he could. His height still startled me. How could it be that he was still growing? Unlike his sister, our easygoing Matthew had slid back into American culture without a hitch. He'd settled quickly into middle school as if he had never left. He boosted himself onto the kitchen counter, his size-fourteen shoes dangling close to the floor.

"Why can't I come to Florence?" Matthew asked as he crunched on croutons.

"You have school."

"And basketball," Katie added with a flip of her blonde ponytail. "And who would watch the dogs?"

"We could bring Zucca. It would be like old times. Come on!" he complained.

"Your time will come. College is just around the corner for you too," I said, pulling a large pot from beneath the stove and placing it in the sink to fill with water.

Matthew grabbed the bag of spicy croutons, threw another handful into his mouth, then turned and breathed his garlic breath into Katie's face. "Ew," she said, pushing him away as he laughed. These were the moments I was going to miss one day—the three of us in the kitchen making dinner while we joked and chatted about the issues du jour. Those endless moments of parenting that I almost drowned in when I was younger but now cherish.

"Can you two set the table? Dad'll be home any minute," I said as I increased the heat of the burner. From the corner of my eye, I saw Matthew spring from the counter to the floor and then up to touch the ceiling again with greasy crouton fingers, leaving tiny marks that I knew I would never want to paint over.

"At least I get to use your car while you're gone," he said. *What if he wraps the car around a lamppost?* "Dad said I could I have friends over on both that Friday and Saturday night." *What if someone sneaks liquor into the house?*

"What else did Dad say?" I asked.

"Just stuff about all these house projects he wants to get done." *House projects? Oh no.* Katie and I exchanged looks of feigned panic, as this conjured memories of a variety of unfortunate decorating decisions that had been made over the years in our absence. Invariably, whenever I am gone for more than two days, Tim gets domestic.

"What kind of projects?" I asked as casually as I could.

"Decorating and fixing stuff. Something about new light fixtures."

Maybe I shouldn't go.

"Just keep the receipts in the desk drawer for me, okay?" I said. We all shared a knowing laugh and pretended I was joking.

"Can we check out the after-Christmas sales this week?" Katie said. "My clothes are all wrong. I need some sort of rain jacket."

"I was thinking the same thing. I'll need to step up my act a little too," I said.

"That's an understatement," mumbled Matthew with a mischievous grin as he gathered silverware extra-noisily on purpose.

I pretended that I was going to swat him with a huge spoon, and he ducked for cover. "I've got some game left," I said.

CHAPTER 4

A Time for Courage

After a long, pensive drive across the desert, I deposited Katie at her friend's house in Pasadena. A small group of students from the study abroad program would be traveling together, and since I was still relegated to ghost-mom status, I had made solo arrangements for the evening. My flight didn't leave until the next day, so I decided to spend it close to the airport, where I could start my journey with a good night's sleep.

I wound through the spaghetti maze of LA highways. It had been a while since I had driven through a blue-sky, California afternoon. I blasted the radio and sang boisterously, not caring that other drivers were giving me sideways glances. My "business trip" was officially beginning, and a surge of excitement rushed through me. I turned into the Airport Marriott on Century Boulevard and parked in the garage. Hoisting my backpack onto one shoulder, I grabbed the extension handle of my rolling suitcase and headed inside.

The check-in counter was buzzing with guests, so I waited patiently while I scanned the lobby's pleasing dark wood furniture and gold walls. A perfectly suitable place for a woman traveling alone to spend an evening.

"May I help you?" A young woman with porcelain skin and hair the color of paprika smiled to reveal perfect teeth.

"I'm checking in," I said as I jockeyed my bags over to the counter. "Pohlman, one night."

With lithe fingers tipped in fuchsia, she typed my information into her computer. "I'll need your credit card," she said. I handed it to her, and she finished the transaction by asking me to sign a paper. She handed me a key card and pointed me to the elevators. "Sixth floor."

An hour later, after checking the closet, fluffing the pillows, laying out my clothes for the morning, unpacking my toiletries, and admiring the view of Century Boulevard and the airport beyond, I decided that a salad and a glass of wine in the bar was exactly what I needed to calm my nerves and ready me for bed. All I needed was some courage or what my mother always referred to as *gumption*.

In my entire life I had never sat alone at a bar unless

I had already arranged to meet someone. I couldn't bear the stereotype of the lonely middle-aged woman looking for Mr. Goodbar. I was bent on breaking new ground, however, and ready to do so. It was the twenty-first century; people were different these days. Women could sit at bars and have a drink without affixing a scarlet letter to their foreheads. Couldn't they? I could bring one of my Florence guidebooks with me as a security measure. It always helps to have something to read.

I put on some lip color, threw my shoulders back, and headed down the long hallway with its carved molding, the patterned carpet springy beneath my feet. The elevator doors opened, and I joined an unshaven balding man in wrinkled khaki pants that matched the pallor of his skin, and a young Asian beauty in a black miniskirt that disappeared under a sheet of ebony hair. Neither would make eye contact with me, so I scrapped any idea of making small talk and pushed the button. The elevator descended to the third floor, and they got off. As the doors closed, I could hear him directing her to a certain room number.

I realized she was a working girl, and I suddenly wondered, with a sick feeling, how many laws were being broken behind these seven floors of locked doors. It's an airport hotel, for goodness' sake! I would have to be careful. My cloud of exhilaration dissipated.

Making my way across the lobby, I decided that if all else failed I could buy a glass of Chardonnay and take it to my room to sip in safety. I entered the bar, Latitude 33, and did the old I'm-looking-for-someone-but-they're-not-here-yet routine. The place was packed—with men. Where were the women? There were no seats at the bar, and the last thing I wanted was to sit at a table by myself. I may as well display a placard that said: *I am alone and vulnerable in my room on the sixth floor.*

A few heads turned in my direction, and I smiled, making sure that my book on Florence was in full view. I hated that I was thinking this way. I usually work on projecting confidence when I am alone in an unexpected situation. I hate that our world has an evil underbelly that instills fear and inhibits a woman's ability to travel alone. How many more of us would take off for parts unknown if we knew that our safety would not be compromised? Every man in this room could be as trustworthy and decent as one of my own brothers, but newspaper headlines of missing persons and grisly crimes flashed before my eyes. Was a glass of wine worth that?

Suddenly, I became fearful. It was not too late to jump in my car and return home. *Maybe I shouldn't go.* There it was again! That nagging voice. I took a deep breath and found a seat trying to remember the last time I was this uncomfortable.

I find it ironic and confusing to know that I can have faith in a God I have never seen, but I won't trust people sitting right in front of me. Though I intellectually understand that fear is the opposite of faith, I wrestle with it every day. I lock my house when I'm home alone, and my car doors when I'm driving. I carry pepper spray and scan crowds like a hired security guard. When I see someone in disarray or exuding an odd energy, I automatically assign them to the unsolved neighborhood crime. Fear is exhausting.

Well, I may not want to go home, but I decided to go back to my room. Grabbing my phone like I had just received an important call, I strode out of the restaurant, crossed the lobby and waited for the elevator. As I pushed the button for the sixth floor, a squat man in a shiny gray suit dashed in and pressed the button for the seventh floor. I leaned against the back wall of the elevator and envisioned how I could take him down if he gave me any guff. When the doors opened, we nodded to each other and I walked, deflated, down the long hallway that now reminded me of *The Shining*, and wondered what had happened to my gumption. I had an opportunity to push myself and, instead, chose the safety of retreat. Other than my own runaway thoughts, I had absolutely no solid reason for it. Fear was a habit that I needed to learn to break. How many experiences had I passed on in life thus far due to a reluctance to trust others? How many times had I let fear steal from me?

Starting tomorrow, I would quash the irrational voices in my head, at least for the next ten days, and push myself. I would be the poster child for gumption. I would be careful and prudent as a woman traveling alone, but I would not be stopped.

Taking the key card from my purse, I looked up and down the hall to make sure I wasn't followed and opened the door. The drapes glowed orange from the setting sun, so I pulled them wide and sat in a straight-backed chair to watch night throw its veil across the city. Dark figures ambled to and fro on the sidewalks below. A raggedy woman in a shapeless overcoat and a maroon knit cap stopped at a garbage can to sift through its contents. Then she wobbled off into the shadows. With a prayer for her safety on my heart, I brushed my teeth, double-locked the door, and climbed into bed.

CHAPTER 5

The Train

The train between Rome's Fiumicino airport and Florence glided over the tracks, steel against steel; the swaying motion a sedative. I peered over my shoulder at the other faces on board. I saw a bright-eyed teen in red heels, a weary young mother corralling two young boys who were slapping at each other with sticky lollipops, a woman in a salmon-colored suit laughing with her curly-haired daughter as she pointed to a headline in the paper, and a silver-haired woman with a travel guide seated alone. Settling into my seat, I realized, as I chewed on the end of my pencil, that all of my eras, the people within me, could fill this train car. It is one of the gifts of aging, to be aware of all the previous stages of your life at once.

I made a list of my great topics of concern at this moment in time. A "seeking guide" I could refer to as I wandered through the next few days:

- How do I help Katie (and soon, Matthew) transition to a life of their own?
- What kind of mother should I become as my children leave the nest?
- Who will I be when my time becomes my own again?
- How do I navigate marriage in this new era?
- How do I discern my "great" purpose in life? Who is God calling me to be?
- My changing body. (Ugh...just, ugh).
- Grief: the loss of family members, friendships that have reached an end, my youth.

Okay, so it was tall order by anyone's standards. At least it felt good to put it on paper. If I could find peace with at least one of these, I'd be satisfied.

Reviewing the list as we rolled along, it dawned on me that none of these were material in nature. I would not find answers in shops and restaurants (though I was afraid I might *accidentally* enjoy them), instead, I set my sights on places marked by human struggle and soulful expression. When I was not helping Katie in some way, I would spend my time seeking answers by visiting places of worship and art galleries. My tools would include photography and journaling and prayer.

Relaxing, I watched the Tuscan countryside whiz by. The backdrop of the winter sky made the passing hilltop villages mysterious and alluring, the large churches that anchored them, all the more grand and imposing. Cities, now, are wrapped around bank buildings and corporate headquarters. I wondered if people's lives had more clarity long ago when faith anchored the community. I wondered if our inner restlessness as individuals and the fractures in our families have grown as America has shifted from faith-based communities with large churches and town squares to cities with enormous skyscrapers that insist we worship the power and glory of commerce instead of God.

The conductor, in his navy suit, made his way down the aisle punching tickets. When he asked for mine, I tried to catch his eye, but he wouldn't look at me. I wanted to grab his hole punch and tell him that he was missing opportunities to engage. Remind him that he was standing in a moment filled with humanity. To see that his train car was full of individual stories unfolding, our paragraphs and chapters blending, brushing against each other. A library of life stories speeding along, one more complex and beautiful than the next.

A train unites life's journeyers. We may be in different ages and stages, but we are all traveling in the same direction. This was another reason I am drawn to travel as a tool for self-understanding. The sight of others awakens sleeping memories, conjuring the faces of my old friends, of hobbies I long ago abandoned, of goals I have set aside. It evoked those fleeting days before I was bumped around by life, when I stood alone with my birth name and thought I held more answers than questions about myself.

Not only does travel awaken this sleeping child inside of me, it allows me the time to sit with her for a while. I need to revisit the person I was before the world told me who to be. Midlife rebirth begins there. Uncovering the layers of life and rediscovering the feral nature gifted to me at birth—a true sense of self. How can we ever hope to find meaningful purpose if we don't know our own blessings and claim aloud our passions and strengths?

I will also have nine more days to encourage Katie to take the risks necessary to live a full and exciting life. I hoped to strike a healthy parenting balance of being there if she needed me, yet not hovering or hindering her ability to make decisions of her own. To be there, yet not be there.

Yes, this plan was shaping up quite nicely. I smiled and gave myself an inner high five for making it to this moment, this day. I was feeling stronger already.

Through the window, the Tuscan countryside passed in a blur, the hard edges of winter softened by the speed of the train. I began to recognize names of towns and caught glimpses of hamlets perched on hill-tops. Because I have lived in so many locations in my life thus far, the word *home* is complicated for me. I was feeling a sense of it now, though, beginning to relax, knowing that I could be myself here. I was headed toward me.

Texts from Home: Part 1

Matthew: Hi Mom. Are you there yet? Where did you hide the Oreos? Caramel fell in the pool. I had to rescue her. She couldn't get out!

Me: Hi Matthew. Landed in Rome a bit ago. Still on the train to Florence. Almost there. Oreos are on bottom shelf of the pantry. You may have to bend over to see them. Keep an eye on Caramel.

Matthew: Mrs. Anderson wants to know if you can make eight dozen homemade cookies and brownies for Sophomore Appreciation Day at school.

Me: (What I want to say: Doesn't Safeway deliver?) Sure, no problem. Love you.

Matthew: Love you too.

Me: On the train to Florence. Just checking in.

Katie: It's only 6 a.m. You just woke us up.
Me: Sorry. Safe flight today. Have fun!
Katie: xoxo zzzzzz

Tim: Hi Honey. Glad you're there safe. All good here. Recession getting worse. Don't use your credit card. Love you. xoxo
Me: Hi Honey. On the train to Florence. Don't worry—I'll just use cash. There are ATMs everywhere. ;) Love you too!

CHAPTER 6

Act Two

Jet-lagged and exuberant, I exited the Hotel de Lanzi and stepped eagerly into the waning light of the Florentine afternoon joining scores of others scurrying down the cobblestoned streets in the shadow of the Basilica di Santa Maria del Fiore, or, more commonly called, the Duomo. A commanding presence, it stood high and fearsome, casting long shadows across the alleyways at odd angles. Dwarfed beside it, I stood and looked upward at its cream and moss-green marble like a child entering Disneyland for the first time.

Katie and her friends would not be landing until the following day, so I had all evening to explore. With the aroma of baking bread on the breeze, I fell into step with the Florentines and tourists who filled the sidewalks. Two grandmothers leisurely pushed baby carriages one-handed, the other hand free to flit about their animated conversation. Three young businessmen strutted with purpose, the collars of their black overcoats turned upright against the cold as they eyed college girls and smoked cigarettes. A stylish older woman, elegant in her brown mink coat, clutched the arm of her husband as they strolled, engaged in an intimate tête-à-tête. Heat rose to my face in a blush of happiness. Why had I stayed away so long?

I peered into confectionary store windows marveling at cookies and chocolates stacked in artful symmetry; stopped at a leather shop to gaze at rainbows of wallets, purses, and belts; and perused a fine stationery store recalling an era when ink came in glass bottles and pens scratched important words onto handmade paper. I strolled by an enoteca filled with friends, glasses of wine raised in celebration and pressed my nose to windows that displayed scarves and fine silks while mounted police dressed in blue capes and white coats rode by, their horses' hooves clomping on the cold stone.

Suddenly, a hand grabbed my arm as I stepped into a crosswalk. Startled, I turned to look, realizing that someone had pulled me from the path of a silver Smart car hurtling past. I looked into the eyes of a blonde-haired man, a plaid scarf wrapped around his neck. "Thank you!" I said as he let go of my arm.

"He almost hit you," said the man. "He shouldn't have been driving that fast. I guess he didn't see you."

"I guess not. I'm getting used to it," I laughed trying to make light of the situation.

"Be careful," he said as he disappeared into the crowd.

The driver hadn't seen me. Invisibility. I'd had numerous discussions with friends regarding this unwelcome phenomenon. After turning forty, we noticed that we began to lose our luster. Not all at once, but in baby steps, where you teeter for a moment and then regain your balance. Like the first time some college kid called me "ma'am." (*What? Who me?*) Or the day a distinguished older man turned his head to regard my daughter as she and I walked a hilly neighborhood in San Francisco. (*What? You're my age. What about me?*)

Then the signs of our fading became more frequent and alarming, warranting middle-of-the-day distress calls to each other or cryptic e-mails and text messages — *I sat in the waiting room at the doctor's office for an hour. They didn't see me.*

Even on a good day, we had become just somebody's mom, adrift at sea in a middle-aged ocean. Though I was beginning to accept my new invisibility status, it still hurt. There is loss involved, so I think we are allowed to grieve; but I was realizing that it was also becoming easier to choose to be invisible. To get lazy. There was a great excuse at my fingertips every time an uncomfortable choice arose. *I'm too old. Past my prime. Who would notice? What do I have left to give? Why should I care?*

Night fell like a whisper, soft and mysterious. My beloved stars appeared overhead, shiny pinpricks in deep-blue velvet. As I ambled toward the lights of the Palazzo Vecchio, Florence's town hall, haunting organ music beckoned from the darkened entryway of a small church, recessed from the street. Through the open door, flickers of candlelight danced in the shadows. If it weren't for the music, I would have walked past it.

Deciding to look inside, I climbed three stone steps worn in the center from a million seeking footsteps across the ages. As my eyes adjusted to the gloom I could see there were side altars illuminated by dim lights. A lone woman huddled in the last pew, her shawl-covered head cradled in her chapped, arthritic hands. In the far-right corner of the front altar, almost hidden by an elaborate manger scene, an organist sat at an ancient pipe organ. He played a simple piece with confidence, the music filling the hidden spaces, both mine and the church's. I walked slowly up and down the side aisles studying frescoes and artwork, the patterned black-and-white marble floor cold and smooth beneath my feet. It was a small and insignificant church compared to the Duomo or Santa Maria Novella, but it felt considerable at the moment.

In the far-left corner facing the pews, a silver-haired man with sad eyes perched on a cane-backed chair. On his lap a small white Scottie sat upright, still as the air around them. I nodded to the man, but he and his dog continued to stare ahead, making no indication that they saw me.

I ducked into one of the hard, wooden pews and knelt to say a prayer of gratitude for my safe journey, for the safe travels of Katie and her friends, and the gift of this trip. From this vantage point I could see that the organist was just a college kid, his two deft hands working the keys with passion, his feet pumping the pedals. Bent forward in concentration, his black hair fell in a curtain over his eyes. What kind of young man plays alone in a musty church on a Tuesday night? What's the glory in that?

However, this young musician already knew what I was just beginning to understand. It didn't matter that all of Florence couldn't hear him. I heard him. He drew me in and inspired me to pray, by simply using the talents with which he has been blessed. We may never know how we touch another heart, but that's the beauty of how we have been created. Each of us longs for something another can provide. I sat with my eyes closed for the next few songs and let the hymns fill me, open me.

Here, in this unlikely place, began the change in my thoughts about middle-aged invisibility. It is a concept born of the marketplace, a by-product of materialism and the obsessive search for creaseless skin. I didn't care, anymore, that an oversized brown cane had yanked me off the stage of youth. That's how it goes. Many of us are blessed with the chance to play a leading role in that production, but not all of us are blessed with a second act. How many men and women would have loved to have lived past thirty, forty, or fifty?

This was my "jumping off point" for my search for purpose in the next chapter of my life. Act Two is about interiority, revealing that which is within. It takes more courage to live from the inside out. It takes a sort of fearlessness to sit on a darkened stage on a cold night and play your music as if you were in Carnegie Hall, though only God and a few passing strangers might hear you. We are not invisible to those who seek our light, yearn for our music, or crave our touch.

I sat for a long while and relaxed into the moment. A sense of relief washed over me like the thaw after a hard winter. Modern culture encases us with layers of shoulds and musts that, in the end, don't often matter. Returning to grace involves a peeling back of these layers and that takes time.

I remembered the line from the classic movie *Field of Dreams*: "If you build it, he will come." Dealing with middle-aged invisibility is sort of the same thing. Live your calling and you will appear. We will never feel more visible than that. The only problem was that I didn't know what that calling was yet. But I had several glorious days ahead to seek for it. Who knew what revelations might come my way.

I looked toward a tree-shaped rack of tea lights flickering before the altar. I lit a candle for all those I loved and placed it on the top tier. The musician began a new piece, its melody both earthly and divine as the old woman, the elderly man, and his dog continued their vigil. I walked down the center aisle, but before I departed, I stood in the nave and turned for one last look around the interior and a final glimpse of the tiny flames in the darkness. Something we all can aspire to be.

CHAPTER 7

Seeking Faith

Since it was right outside my hotel door, my first mission was to tackle the Duomo. This massive cathedral, with its famed mosaic floor and frescoed ceilings, sits in the historic center of Florence. Over eighty-nine thousand square feet at its base, its dome reaches four hundred feet into the air. I had walked around the Duomo a few times last evening to unwind before I turned in for the night, but it was now time to venture inside. Though last night's inspiring experience in the church I happened upon was unexpected, I had planned to begin the week with a meditation about faith and its place in my life. If I wanted to find balance and meaningful direction in midlife, I needed to start with God. I needed to get real with my beliefs and my questions. Faith anchors a life of meaning.

The first time I toured the Duomo a few years ago, the experience was unexpectedly emotional. I'm not usually a crier in churches and museums, but I wept as I walked through it and marveled at the art and grandeur. I didn't understand why I'd had such a visceral reaction, but I knew that I would be back one day to explore it. So, prior to this trip, I decided to do some research. I wanted to know more about what I was viewing. After finding the basic information about the building on the Internet, I went deeper and ventured into *The Lives of the Artists* by Giorgio Vasari, an Italian painter, architect, writer, and historian. (The frescoes on the ceiling of the Duomo, depicting heaven and hell, were designed by Vasari.)

Entering and walking through the central nave, the immensity of the building does two things: it makes me feel small, and it insists that I look up. The walls are a plain cream and grey which only accentuate the brilliant colors of the frescoes above. With my head tilted back and my eyes upward, Vasari's praise of Filippo Brunelleschi, the architect who designed the dome that topped the Duomo, echoed in my head, "Many men are created by nature small in person and in features, who have a mind full of such greatness and a heart of such irresistible vehemence, that if they do not begin difficult—nay, almost impossible—undertakings, and bring them to completion to the marvel of all who behold them, they have never any peace in their lives; and whatsoever work chance puts into their hands, however lowly and base it may be, they give it value and nobility."

Vasari put into words what the Duomo proves about the potential that lies within us. His words are a powerful tribute to Brunelleschi, an ordinary man who began his career as a goldsmith and ended it, after discovering and following his true passion for mathematics and architecture, with the revolutionary achievement of the design and construction of this immense dome.

When they first started work on the cathedral, the engineering know-how required to build a dome of this size without internal scaffolding didn't exist. Unbelievably, they just left a big, gaping hole in the roof and waited for someone to come along and figure it out. Who builds a cathedral with unfinished plans and hopes that someone else will figure it out? I could not imagine that happening in this day and age. Florentines waited over a hundred years before they held a competition to find someone who could design the dome. A competition!

Before Brunelleschi decided to enter the competition to solve the problem, he stated with surety to the construction team: "This is a temple consecrated to God and to the Virgin, I am confident, since this is being done in memory of her, that she will not fail to infuse knowledge where it is lacking, and to give strength, wisdom, and genius to him who is to be the author of such a work."

Brunelleschi didn't know that it was going to be *him*. That he would, ultimately, be the inspired author. I think his great faith was rewarded. It wasn't easy for him, though. When the time came for him to stand before the panel of judges and reveal his proposed engineering strategy, they scoffed at him "deriding him with mocking laughter… that this was the plan of a madman, as he was." However, inspired and undeterred, Brunelleschi pushed on, meeting individually with the various men in charge and showed them his models and drawings, until, eventually, he was given permission to proceed. What if he had given up due to their laughter and mockery?

After walking a bit and acclimating to the space, I decided to challenge myself and climb to the top of the dome. There are 463 steps to the top and, according to all the guidebooks, the view from the top was a "must see." I could guess what the view was going to look like —red tile roofs, countryside in the distance—but guessing what something will be like isn't usually as good as doing it.

I walked to a small booth where a stern-faced guard explained that there were four sets of stairs that spiraled from the ground level through the great piers that supported the dome. Part of the original construction, the workers used them to transport materials. Two were for the workers going up and two were for the workers coming down, to avoid opposing traffic. He assured me that the whole journey would take only about twenty minutes.

"Sounds good," I said plopping a few euros onto the counter. I would do this in honor of Brunelleschi and all the other geniuses who are roaming the earth yet to be discovered. Entering the stairwell, I passed a sign that warned people with heart conditions to turn around, and another that asked that we don't write on the walls.

The stairwell was a narrow, somber passageway with worn steps and walls made of huge stone blocks. Ten steps up, turn on a small landing, another ten steps up, turn on a small landing. Easy schmeasy. Imagining a princess wearing a flowing chiffon gown gracefully ascending in beaded slippers in search of her prince, I passed a few narrow glassless windows, open rectangles like gun turrets, through which a watery light seeped. When I stopped and stood on tiptoes to peer through one, I caught a glimpse of the red-tiled tops of neighboring buildings.

The risers between the steps became unusually steep. My thighs strained. Were the walls closing in a little? I looked down at my feet as I climbed, limiting my senses. I didn't like this idea anymore. All of a sudden, I had to inhale extra-deeply. Then, again. So, I loosened my scarf and unbuttoned my jacket.

I passed through short corridors with countless names scrawled on the walls in marker and ink. So much for the sign at the entrance. Why do people feel compelled to put their names on such a world treasure? In my mind's eye, I dipped a roller in a bucket of white paint and rolled right over them. The only names allowed here should be those who built the place, the hundreds of dedicated artisans and workers who made endless journeys up and down these stairs. Though their names are unknown to the world, I think their signatures float and drift endlessly in the air, their might and sweat and indomitable spirit as much a part of the structure as the brick and stone.

I glanced at my watch. It felt like I had been in here a lot longer than five minutes. I turned another corner and started up a spiral staircase that would have thrilled Alfred Hitchcock. I put both hands out to steady myself, as there was barely room for one foot on each triangular step. Up and up I went. Dizzying panic rose in my throat. I have had only one full-blown panic attack in my life, I didn't want my second to occur here. The spirals lasted too long. Just when I thought I would burst into tears, a landing—then up another spiral, then another, then another.

I remembered the safe and secure feeling of walking outside, circling the Duomo last night and this morning. Then I thought about the joy of entering the cathedral at ground level to enjoy the artwork and architecture within feet of an exit. Now, committed to exploring the intricacies of the inner workings of the structure, things weren't so glamorous.

Like my personal journey of faith, it is much easier to circle my beliefs at a distance and proclaim their beauty than it is to get inside of them and climb. The climbing part: the reading and study of scripture; the examination and acceptance of religious doctrine and ceremony; the consistent participation in services and fellowship require persistence and obedience (two qualities I am not particularly great at). It is easy to choose the path of least resistance, and thus, easy to fall away from faith.

Especially now, in the era of church cover-ups and failed leadership, it is difficult to maintain enthusiasm. The hierarchy has never seemed more human. It is easy to wonder what is real and what is false. It is easy to question with disgust. It is easy and understandable to panic when the spirals last too long and our footing becomes less sure. In the end, faith is both a gift and a choice. Do I choose to keep climbing toward enlightenment or retreat into comfort?

My very-close-together, extra-deep breaths began again. Looking behind me, I could see that the stairs were too narrow for me to turn back. I could picture other tourists on their way up trying to make way for a screaming maniac pushing against them to get down. Where the heck was the top of this thing?

Another narrow window appeared around the next bend. Balancing on tiptoes on a tiny pie slice of stone stair, I put my face in front of it. I was so high that all I could see was the sky, a shade lighter than the gunmetal stone.

A few more deep breaths to get a grip on myself, then up more spirals, silent but for the slap of my leather soles against stone. Finally, I stepped out onto a clear acrylic-sided walkway inside the perimeter of the top of the dome. I was relieved and petrified at the same time. The same feeling as breaching the apex of your first roller coaster. The open air provided breathing room, but the fact that it was four hundred feet above the floor turned my legs to jelly. I chanced a look downward and wondered which of the teeny-tiny people I would squash when I fell.

I put my hand against the dome, eye to eye with Vasari and Zuccari's fresco, *The Last Judgment*. Perfect subject matter. I was suddenly among the undeserving, trying to dodge the devils and climb toward heaven.

For the first time in my life, height overwhelmed me. I could not enjoy even one brushstroke. The racing of my heart and the beating of the blood in my ears blinded me. I cupped my hands to shield my eyes like I was a skittish horse with blinders and fixed my sights on a door at the end of the walkway.

I expected to open the door and step into fresh air. Instead, the opening took me back inside a curved labyrinth of space that was in-between the two domes of the structure. This had been Brunelleschi's brilliance: two domes, one inside the other. Ridiculous, they had said. Preposterous. And now, hundreds of years later, I was standing inside them.

Ridiculous, they had said about Christ, preposterous. Yet hundreds of years later I am still standing inside His words.

At last I ascended steps number 461, 462, and 463, and then a ladder that steered me through a hatch-like door. I stood on the balcony at the base of the dome's lantern—the small cupola-like structure mounted on top of the dome—with a gasp of relief and awe. Scooting behind other tourists, I pressed my back against the wall. Once anchored, I gulped the air and calmed myself.

Yes, a patchwork of the red-tiled rooftops of Florence and the lush Tuscan countryside stretched in every direction. Sunlight broke through the clouds and, for a golden moment, showered the hilltop Etruscan city of Fiesole and flashed off the Arno River.

At least I was right about something—guessing what it would be like was nowhere close to standing here and seeing it firsthand. The climb had been worth it. The climb, it seems, is always worth it. The climb, though dizzying and tough at times, takes us closer to heaven.

The people on the streets scurried like black ants, and the street noise dissipated somewhere below. Birds flew at eye level, and I felt a stirring mixture of freedom and fear. When I felt steady, I did one lap around the dome to admire each vantage point.

Stunning, astonishing, magnificent—no words

could capture the experience. I thought of how Brunelleschi must have felt when he stood upon this spot and watched the last brick drop into place. Like the herringbone pattern of the bricks on the dome beneath me, I marveled again how passion plus faith had accomplished the impossible.

Passion and faith are a potent combination, and I tucked an encouraging thought into my heart: We should not be afraid of pursuing our dreams even if we do not know all the answers. If we are called to a task, if we consecrate our work to God—we will be led. Inspirational people will appear along the way to help us, and any one of us can be one of those inspired people for others. Vasari's words about Brunelleschi can apply to any of us: "small and insignificant in appearance . . . souls filled with such greatness . . . hearts with such boundless courage."

I asked a friendly Italian fellow, Lorenzo, to snap my picture. Then, because he was so handsome, and I wanted to stare at him some more, I cajoled him into taking another lap around the top, so I could have backgrounds in the photos from each direction.

"Grazie, Lorenzo. Devo andare." *I must go.*

"Ciao, belle donne! Fare attenzione." *Be careful.*

I ducked back into the dome and began my descent. Though still uncomfortable, it was much easier. I had traveled this path and knew where it would lead. I scurried along the curve of the ceiling, spiraled down Hitchcock's alley, and made another loop through the inside of the dome, this time on a more manageable ledge halfway down. I gave a nod to God, Jesus, and the twelve apostles looking down at me from the fresco.

This climb reminded me that endurance is important. The journey of faith requires stamina. Choosing to continue to climb over and over again is the important thing. I may sit on a step here and there to rest when life overwhelms me or world events create a fog of disillusionment, but the choice to move forward and upward can create opportunities for God to work through us. Opportunities to help others.

Brunelleschi was in his forties when he designed this dome. He was more than halfway through his life (he died at sixty-nine) before he came to know his true calling. Before he accomplished something amazing.

So, it was quite possible that my best days were ahead.

CHAPTER 8

A Time to Let Go - Part 1

Heading down Via Ghibellina, I searched the numbers on the buildings for Katie's address. Before leaving the States, we had planned to meet this afternoon. I was eager to see her. I had no idea what to say to her, or not say, I only knew that I had to get it right in order to boost her confidence; help her feel her own power.

The streets in this part of town were narrow and dark, barely illuminated by a thin strip of cloudy sky between the rooftops. The timeworn buildings, faded mustard and khaki, were smudged from exhaust and marred by the occasional insult of graffiti. Cars were parked bumper to bumper on one side of the street. Unlike the touristy thoroughfares close to the Duomo, this was a real neighborhood, with a sense of privacy and depth. Lives were being lived here, family stories being written. An aproned woman sweeping a stoop. A little boy's face in the window. A grocer filling a crate with onions. A stray black cat.

While walking, I trailed my fingertips across the flat fronts of the buildings and then along the dusty glass of a small coffee shop. I felt the need to touch the walls that would watch Katie walk to and from her classes. Would the owner of the coffee shop look out for her? Probably not. American students come and go.

I was entrusting my sweet girl to these streets, this stone. I was counting on Florence to wrap its charms around her and keep her from harm. It was a big city, though, and I knew about big-city issues. Regardless of culture, human nature is human nature. Bad things can happen.

Far more often than not, however, the things that happen are good. Even better than good. A myriad of sounds is waiting to be heard, a multitude of flavors are waiting to be tasted, and laughter is waiting to be shared.

I located the address and pressed a glossy black button under her apartment number. Housing both students and townspeople, the building was not a dormitory. A loud buzz unlocked the heavy door, and I pushed inward. Entering a shadowy foyer, I saw that the elevator had an OUT OF SERVICE notice on it. I blew a layer of dust off the sign and smiled. Knowing Katie was on the fourth floor, I headed up the stairs.

Rounding the last corner, I saw her lean frame silhou-etted in a doorway that opened into a bright apartment. She wore faded jeans and the blue crewneck sweater that her grandmother had knitted her one year for her birthday. Her hair hung in blonde ringlets still wet from a shower.

"Hi, Mom," she said as I gave her a big hug.

"Hi, honey." She smelled of shampoo and fatigue.

"Well, we made it," she said as she led me into a large open space that was a combination living room/kitchen/dining area. A white tile floor and freshly painted white walls gave it a modern feel. It would be just fine. "It didn't go exactly as planned," she continued. "Our flight was delayed in Munich, so no one from the school met us at the airport. We split a cab, and the driver had a hard time fitting our luggage in the trunk. When we got here, the elevator was broken, and Will had to lug all of our suitcases to the apartment, because Laura and I couldn't even lift them."

"Poor guy," I said, picturing him with Katie and Laura's monstrous suitcases. Like dragging a couple of hippos up four flights.

"I know." She smiled as she nodded. "He wasn't thrilled about it. I thought he was going to faint."

"I'm happy he's here," I said. By some stroke of fate that I suspected was secretly orchestrated by Katie, Will had scored a place with four other guys on the floor below. It brought us enormous comfort, as he was the boyfriend that all parents wished for their daughters.

"It's a great apartment," I said. "The kitchen is perfect." We took a ten-second tour of the fridge and oven and agreed that she was darn lucky.

"Our other roommates are friendly. You'll meet them later," she said. "One's a writer. Another is a chef. Not sure about the third."

"Words and food, my two favorite subjects." We laughed. As she led me down a short hallway to her room, the wood floors creaked beneath my feet. It was spacious, with twin beds and a window that opened onto a maze of alleys and red tile roofs. "Laura's already unpacked, but I wanted to wait for you."

"I'm glad you did," I said, my heart skipping a beat. It was my first clue. A crack in the veneer.

"There's plenty of storage."

"Here. I'll hand you things, and you can place them where you want," I offered. We unpacked her clothes one by one, and she arranged them in a large armoire that stood against the wall. She was our nester, always searching for order. Demanding it. How many times had we done this together? Moving to a new home, creating her room, arranging her living space. Safe and secure, Katie fashion.

I swallowed a familiar lump of guilt about the eleven times we relocated her over the years. Eleven bedrooms to call her own. Her nature was one that likes to burrow, and we pushed her to hunt and roam. Through the years, I kept convincing myself that it's important to know how to do both. But, maybe it's not. What do I know? I enjoyed the same bedroom for the first twenty-four years of my life.

She arranged and rearranged her sweaters, stacking them first on the bottom shelf and then the middle. Her sighs became louder, her breaths deeper. The skin around her eyes tightened, and her jaws clenched and unclenched. Then she began to unpack things that I didn't remember being on her extensive list back home. Hidden between her scarves and underwear were trepidation and distress; apprehension was tucked among her T-shirts and shoes; dread was pressed between the pages of her books; and stuffed inside a boot was good old-fashioned worry.

When she took a handful of DVDs and whatnots and slapped them into an unorganized heap on her bedside table, I knew we were heading toward meltdown. With darting eyes and pursed lips, she sat on the bed next to me. We both gazed out the window. A radiator hissed.

"How's your hotel?" she asked.

"When I arrived, there was a folded piece of white paper taped to the door with my name on it, written in pencil," I said.

"No," she gasped. "Not really."

"Really. The note sent me to another hotel around the corner. Supposedly, they were doing renovations." We shook our heads and laughed. "The new hotel is fine. It won't win any awards, but it's clean and two blocks from the Duomo."

"I don't know about this view," she said with a sweep of her hand toward the window. "It's so crowded. All those rooftops, so many alleyways. I hope I don't get lost down there."

"This," I said, pointing to the neighborhood adjacent to her new home, "is visual poetry. Granted, it's not the Mediterranean, but soon you'll be able to read the time according to how the sun shines on the tiles. You'll fall in love with it."

"I don't think so," she said as she took a sock and wiped the dust from the windowsill. "Mom?"

"Yes?" I asked, knowing what was coming. "What if I can't do this?"

"Then you can come home. You're only a plane ride away. Remember what we used to say when we lived here and had no idea what we were doing?"

"Yes."

"What?" I nudged her to say it with me.

"What's the worst that can happen?" we said in unison.

"You have a credit card," I continued, "and you know how to get to the airport."

"It would be embarrassing," she said.

"Embarrassment is not life-threatening."

"It's crazy. I lived here for a year, I know the language, and still . . . I'm so afraid, and I don't even know what I'm afraid of," she admitted. Transition, transformation, change. It doesn't matter if we are five, fifteen, or fifty, it never gets easier. One of the upsides of our many relocations, however, is that it has given our family plenty of practice in understanding the process of change.

"You always settle in," I said.

"I know it in my head, but I don't feel it yet," she mumbled as she searched for a Kleenex. Katie stood, blew her nose, and resumed her unpacking. Could I have done this when I was her age? I didn't come from a family culture of seeing the world. We were the sort of family that saw the neighborhood. We never considered that we might see the moon rise over the Arno River. We were the type of family that rented a rickety lake cottage in Maine for two weeks in July and giggled with pleasure at our bounty.

Are kids more sophisticated these days, or do we just push them further before they are ready? Truth be told, I would probably have been petrified. I glanced around the room to distract myself, in hopes that I wouldn't cry.

Standing before her armoire, as her hands arranged and rearranged her things, I didn't see her as my child, but as a young woman called to teach the world a few lessons of her own. She was Esther being prepared for holy work for "such a time as this." I realized that as much as I was raising my children, so were they raising me.

Katie has taught me a lot about bravery. Not just the watch-me-try-something-new sort of bravery, but also the pull-myself-off-the-floor-and-take-one-step sort of bravery. She has always been one to name her fears and vulnerabilities. She paints the picture of her heart and soul in words for all to hear, loud and clear. Maybe it's generational, but I have never been one to assert my fears or share my angst. I was the child who was taught to listen, to go along with the group, never to challenge or upset. My voice had always been the one that agreed, that smoothed the ruffled feathers, that sought the humor and kept the peace. I am the keep-your-mouth-shut-and-soldier-on sort of person, but as time passes, I am realizing that my tendency to not speak my mind can hinder more than help. It is not only a habit, or a well-ingrained coping mechanism; it is cowardly. It's not the way I want to finish my life. I want a voice. I want to stir the pot, and that will take chutzpah, because I have run from conflict all of my life. That's not to say I haven't stood to fight when it was worth it; it just means I sidestep a lot. I'm growing weary of that sideways dance.

Katie is not a sidestepper. She walks, eyes wide, straight into battle, and it is why she has been able to accomplish things that many could not. I have watched her choose lofty goals with the full knowledge and expectation that the process would bring her angst and anxiety. She understands that the road to change is riddled with potholes. When she chooses a vision for herself, she sticks with it. Some will call it stubborn-ness, but I call it willpower. While she verbalizes her anxiety, while her body may tremble, and her eyes may tear from time to time, her willpower walks boldly on until her vision takes root and blossoms into happiness and fulfillment. She has already begun to understand that courage is about embracing vulnerability.

I have a handmade tile on my desk at home that Katie gave me for Mother's Day when we were living in Genoa-Nervi. There was an artist who made ceramics in a little shop at the bottom of our hill, and Katie went into her shop and ordered a hand-painted tile with one of her favorite quotes by Mary Anne Radmacher:

Courage is the little voice at the end of the day that says I'll try again tomorrow.

I especially love it because Katie wrote the quote on paper for the artist to copy and misspelled the word tomorrow as *tommorrow*. Spelling has never been her strong point. We laughed about it then, and I smile every time I see it.

Katie stacked her towels and toiletries in her arms and headed to the bathroom. "Mom? Forgot to tell you about this one. You'd better come look," she called from down the hall. I peeked around the corner, and there she stood, in the shower, one wall of which sported a four-by-three-foot clear glass window, suspiciously centered mid-body.

"Only in Italy," I said. "Interesting how this apartment wasn't rented to the boys," I added.

"Not really." She laughed and pointed out the window. "It's pretty obvious. See that window over there? That's someone's kitchen table!"

Thank goodness for humor, the most effective segue on the planet. "Let's get out for a bit. Coffee, and the outdoor market for curtains. How does that sound?"

"Perfect," she said. We grabbed our jackets, headed down the stairs, crossed the street, and entered the coffee shop I had passed on my way here. Katie ordered two cappuccinos and crostatas with the ease of a local. The owner complimented her on her accent. She was going to be fine.

We carried our white porcelain cups and saucers to a small table by the window and sat squarely on the brink of a brand-new chapter in our lives, both afraid of the unknown but drawn inexplicably forward. Katie had lessons to learn here, and so did I. I could offer her advice from my life experience, and she could show me the power of sheer guts.

All of us are each other's bridges to a more heroic self. Youth plus wisdom can change the world. It's one of life's great mysteries that they never arrive in the same package. You only get them one at a time.

Texts from Home: Part 2

Matthew: Hi, Mom. I can't find my basketball jersey. Do you know where it is?

Me: I would guess on the floor of your closet or under your bed. You'll probably have to bend your knees to see it.

Matthew: K. Say hi to Katie. I think Zucca ate some candy. He has the big D.

Me: How did Zucca get the candy?

Matthew: Did you have gelato yet?

Me: Not yet.

Matthew: What is your problem?

Me: I know! Soon. I promise.

Matthew: Mrs. Tunney wants to know if you will do morning carpool for her all of March.

Me: (What I want to say: Why can't Mr. Tunney do it instead?) Sure! No problem. Love you.

Matthew: Love you too.

Tim: Hi, honey. How's Katie? How's her place?

Me: Katie is fine. A little wobbly. Place is perfect. Wish you were here!

Tim: Give her a hug for me. Wish I was there, too, though I know you are lying. :)

Me: (silence)

Tim: Work sucks. Everyone is nervous about the economy.

Me: One day at a time, right? Deep breath.

Tim: I love you.

Me: Love you, too.

CHAPTER 9

Santa Croce - Part 1

The iron-colored stone of the Piazza di Santa Croce spread before me pitched and uneven, like it had been painted with thick oil paint applied with a giant palette knife. The gray-and-white facade of the Basilica di Santa Croce, the largest Franciscan church in the world, rose, flat as a postcard, at its far edge. In warm weather, this piazza teemed with artists and café tables, but at this hour in the off-season, there were only pigeons to keep me company. After I dropped Katie at her apartment for a nap, I decided to walk here to sit in the basilica and journal for a while. The basilica and the old monastery grounds that surround it are ideal places for introspection and meditation.

I crossed the piazza with a small army of cooing

friends in tow and headed around the left side of the church to the door. I was almost afraid to enter. Afraid to break the spell of memory that had settled like a lustrous pearl in the folds of my being. I had first come here when it meant nothing more to me than an entry in a guidebook. I had mistakenly assumed it was "just" a church. I didn't realize that it was used as a tomb, a pantheon for the Florentine elite. I didn't know of the power within its walls, or that I would exit a changed person.

I headed inside. Doused in the cavernous space, the sound of my footsteps swept away like a mother's hush. There was texture to this air, heavy and dark near the floor. Filtered light from narrow, stained-glass windows lining the upper half of the building cast the illusion of a rising mist, which demanded an upward gaze. I breathed in the aroma of reverence.

Standing in the rear to get my bearings, I studied the austere beauty of the Franciscan aesthetic. I didn't remember the architectural details of the building as much as I remembered the emotion it stirred, the way it altered the way I understood the boundaries of possibility, the definition of strength.

Santa Croce was modeled after the Cross of Tau, the symbol of Saint Francis of Assisi, which resembles a person with outstretched arms. A series of high pointed arches marches up either side of the basilica, beneath which are individual funerary altars, the final resting place for some of the most brilliant minds of the

Renaissance: Michelangelo, Galileo, Rossini, and Machiavelli, to name a few. In contrast to the tranquil creams and grays of the stone and marble, the wood-beamed ceiling is magnificent unto itself. The vast space of the church is a wonder of order and symmetry —rectangles, triangles, full and half circles working together with harmonious ease. A few rows of stern wooden pews sat up front near the main altar.

The floor is a patchwork of rectangular, white marble sepulchral slabs. Grave sites all. Some were arranged side by side and some alone, cordoned off in the center of the room. Etched names and dates were worn and often unreadable. It irked me that a man in a rumpled Nike sweat suit was strolling across the graves like they were linoleum tiles on his kitchen floor.

Santa Croce calls me to examine the nature of greatness. Makes me stand before it like a mirror and wonder if greatness has passed me by. A few years ago, when I had become viscerally aware that my life had a not-so-distant end point, I began to worry about it. Would I ever do something great? Would I leave a mark? A quiet sadness had seized me as I feared I might quietly leave this world like a puff of smoke that disappeared on the nearest breeze.

I walked from one altar to the next, absorbing the details of the polished marble and sculpture that adorned each sarcophagus. Every name conjured a life marked by brilliance, but I was too experienced, now, to limit my view of them to a label as simple as painter, sculptor, scientist, writer, or composer. I knew too much of the world to regard these masters in the romantic notion that brilliance was straightforward. That their lives were easy.

Galileo called his ideas *theories*. Most others at the time called them *heresy*. Astronomers doubted him. The Inquisition put him on trial and, ultimately, under house arrest. Machiavelli was cursed by many over the centuries for having the gall to shine a light on our human darkness. Rossini suffered from neurasthenia, a mental disorder with psychosomatic symptoms. Yet he was able to compose some of the most entertaining and popular operas ever known.

I stood for a long time at Michelangelo's altar. He was the first to be buried here, and I was struck by the small size of his tomb. It put his humanity in perspective. Though his artwork defined an era, he, too, had his share of tragedy and personal challenge. According to biographer Paolo Giovio, he lost his mother as a child and grew to be an awkwardly social adult. "His nature was so rough and uncouth that his domestic habits were incredibly squalid, and deprived posterity of any pupils who might have followed him." His work demanded a solitary existence. Michelangelo himself wrote, "I am here in great distress and with great physical strain, and have no friends of any kind, nor do I want them; and I do not have enough time to eat as much as I need; my joy and my sorrow, my repose are these discomforts."

The thought of all the many accomplishments represented in this one building overwhelms me. How all of these people created works that changed the order of things, set the world on fire, brought beauty and inspiration and song. It made me wonder what was wrong with me. I had a life, didn't I? One single life, like they did. But where were my accomplishments? What did I have to show for myself, for my one precious life? I felt like I had failed somehow, already.

For some time now, I have chewed on the nature of greatness. I carefully watch those I regard as powerful, potent, and impressive. I study the talented, the resplendent, and the accomplished. It has become one of my private obsessions. I often feel like everyone else's greatness simply illuminates my own lack of it.

I looked around the expanse of the basilica and took a deep breath, imagining what it would be like to sit with these artists now. I would look each one straight in the eye and say, "I know what you accomplished, but how did you do it? What kept you going? What pushed you forward when you wanted to declare defeat? What separates the ordinary person from the extraordinary one?"

Wanting to steep in these thoughts for a while, I walked to the front of the church and sat in the last pew, behind a class of art students who were scratching notes as fast as their learned teacher could expound about stained glass and the frescoed masterpieces of Giotto. A beam of sunshine from a round window high above the front altar gleamed like a spotlight on two intent students in the front row. I could see my own children in their smooth faces and lean, strong bodies. I knew that Katie would be sitting in those pews in the coming weeks, feeling the exhilaration of all things new. I hoped the same for Matthew a few years hence.

The teacher asked a complicated question, and I smiled to myself as the students looked everywhere but at her. It was clear that no one wanted to attempt an answer.

"Try," she demanded. "The answer is right in front of you. Look with new eyes." They remained quiet for the longest time. When the silence became unbearable, a hand rose. A blond waif of a boy with translucent skin and unkempt hair stood. I noticed a few students give each other sideways glances and eye rolls. He saw them, too, and drew in a long breath to steady himself. A blush crawled up his neck, and I willed it to stop, rooting for him. He cleared his throat and threw out a guess in a wavering and unsure voice. By the look on the teacher's face, his answer was far from correct. A muffled snicker rose from somewhere. After another interminable silence, the teacher—bless her wise heart —said, "You know, it doesn't really matter what the answer is. What matters is that you took that chance when no one else had the guts. That was great."

That was great. That was a *moment* of greatness. Right here on display. He took a chance, opening himself to risk. Greatness started there. The boy sat down and smiled. After a few moments, the teacher continued her lesson, gently guiding the students toward the answer, teaching them to look at something in a new way.

I suspect that the human definition of greatness differs from God's definition. We have been conditioned to see greatness in the context of comparison. Measuring a person's individual accomplishments as proof that they were greater than another. It's one big human contest that nobody will ever win. I vowed to stop all of this measuring. If I continued to compare myself to others, I would always feel less than. If I continued to wait until I was sure of something before I tried it, I'd wait a long time. If I continued to wait for another's permission to look into my own light, I would never be among the type of souls that might be buried in a church that forces others to look upward to a bigger sense of themselves.

We may not all be blessed with brilliance, but we are all capable of moments of greatness. We are all capable of heeding that small voice that says we are going in the right direction, even when the world insists otherwise. Capable of choosing right over wrong, bravery over cowardice, forgiveness over hatred. Standing for justice even when we stand alone. Accomplishment is the sum of a long string of great moments and ceaseless toil.

St. Paul, in 2 Corinthians, reminds us that "the exceeding greatness of the power may be of God, and not from ourselves." That we are the "earthen vessels" through which God will express himself if we allow him to work through us.

These words became real to me during the experience of writing my first book, *Halfway to Each Other*. It was the first time in my writing journey that I began each writing session with a prayer and meditation on surrender. I would say the prayer of St. Francis and ask God to use me as an instrument of peace. The material poured out of me, and I could sense God working through me. Now, it's not to say that I didn't plug away at constant rewrites to get the manuscript into shape for publication, but my passion and drive never waned. I experienced a deeper reverence and awe of God's power and the joy that comes from the Holy Spirit working within me.

Like the young organist in that tiny chapel who played his heart out, we are born with a set of talents that may serve a divine purpose that we will never fully understand. Only a few of us will be judged as genius and world-changing by human standards, but all of us might be judged as world-changing by God's standards if we embrace our gifts as part of God's divine providence. Like a pebble tossed into a pond, who knows the ripple that one moment of greatness can affect? Who knew that I would include this moment in a future manuscript?

Delightfully and sufficiently unnerved, I rose from the pew and did one more lap around the church. This next phase of life should be the time to raise my hand

and stand. To take a chance. At something. Midlife and midstream, I must look with new eyes, listen with new ears, and follow the voice that calls to me from within. I want to leave this world, whenever the good Lord decides to take me, with the knowledge and satisfaction that I, indeed, took risks to achieve something great.

CHAPTER 10

Santa Croce - Part 2

I exited the basilica through the side door, and stepped into the *primo chiostro*, the first cloister, a large rectangular swath of lawn with stately cypress trees like tall green fingers. This interior courtyard, designed for the original monastery, was lined with covered walkways, the roofs supported by columns in straight rows. There was a soft breeze, crisp and fresh, stirring the air of this sacred place where the brown robes and sandaled feet of the Franciscan monks quietly padded through life centuries ago. I continued past Baccio Bandinelli's renowned sculpture, Dio Padre, *God the Father*, and continued through the next archway into the second cloister.

Originally comprising the dormitories of the friary, the second cloister is composed of two stories of arched covered walkways on all four sides. The court-yard was a small square-shaped section of grass with an old stone well in center. Above the well was an ornate black wrought-iron cross. The high walls blocked the street noise, and I was treated to a heavenly silence punctuated only by the occasional coo of a pigeon. Wisps of clouds curled in lazy patterns across the sky.

The cloister was another study in symmetry. A place with such history and beauty is always alive with lessons. I scanned the courtyard noting details and colors—searching, now, for a metaphor. I grabbed my camera and ambled about, taking photos of the arched walkways at odd slants. Sometimes, unexpected angles reveal striking images.

I have long marveled at the arches in Italy. Some are plain and sturdy, providing pathways and portals. Others are ornate, boasting artwork that beckons me from across large piazzas. I love them all. They are structures you can count on. So common here that you could walk all day and perceive them as ordinary, dismissing them as a mere backdrop to a garden or as a functional covered walkway. But I love their quiet strength, their rounded backs supporting the weight of cathedrals like Atlas carrying the world.

The arches have done their jobs day in and day out for centuries as sure as the sun and moon have appeared in a celestial arc above them. Over all else, I appreciate the brilliantly simple underlying principle of enduring strength: the arch requires all of its elements, all of its forces, to hold it together to create equilibrium. Take out one piece, one stone block, and it will collapse, taking all that was built upon it down in a crumbled heap.

No offense to the amazing and beautiful men in our lives, but I regard women as the arches in our world. We are beings of enduring strength—supporting families, friends, whole communities. Some people dismiss us as ordinary, a backdrop, the one who cooks and cleans and sends out birthday cards. I know there are exceptions to every rule, but I dare to be bold by saying we are, as a gender, as steadfast as the sun and moon.

Because we innately understand all that rests upon us, we tend to ignore our midlife angst. We tiptoe through our own darkness, so we don't wake anyone else. We tend to dismiss yearnings until they go away. How could we ever handle being the cog that leaves the wheel unable to turn? Such is the need to suppress our fears, our deep shifts, our loneliness or longing to express that which we have ignored for decades. What do we do when we know that we are the stone block in the arch wiggling its way loose? What if we know we are falling apart?

Some people are lucky. Born with the gift of knowing themselves in their youth, they choose paths that make sense their whole life long. Most of us don't, however. We panic around age twenty-three and choose a career because the life-skills test at the counselor's office said we were suited for marketing, nursing, or court stenography. We make it work. We clock in, work hard, and become entangled in the lives of those in the cubicles next to ours. We share laughs and some tears and assure each other that we are lucky to be working there.

Years pass, and we get married or not, and, well, things become busy, and life is expensive, and perhaps there are children to raise and educate, or struggling family members to support. And then there's retirement to think of. So, we continue to work at that good job, feeling thankful—because we are. Then, all of a sudden, on a rainy Thursday afternoon or driving home from the grocery store for the fourth time in a week we realize that there are more days behind us than before us. That's when doubt and fear rent space in our souls and begin to badger us with the ever-seductive list of what-ifs.

Then we might choose to take the long way to work sometimes, maybe stopping under a spreading maple on a spring morning to sneak a cup of coffee and dream of other things. We stare off into space when our boss is doing her best to inspire us, but we don't hear her, because in our minds we are opening boutiques, writing novels, designing perfect living spaces, or building orphanages in Nicaragua.

So, we have a mid-life crisis, or we fight with our

spouses and partners about boredom and routine or enroll in a night class and dabble with something we have always wanted to do. We test the waters by slowly telling others who express surprise that this old curmudgeon has taken to writing poetry, or that accountant has begun to design kites, or that surgeon has taken to the mountain roads on the fastest motor-cycle he can find. Then our little sideshow starts to poke its way into our every day until we realize, one night when we can't sleep, that the sideshow is supposed to be the main act.

I recall that moment, vividly. The tightness in my chest and the nausea that rose from my stomach, because I felt that my life's path had not been the right one. I sat straight upright in the darkness and wanted to declare that this wasn't right at all. Forty-five of my best years rolling along on a road parallel to the proper route. I loved stories and words, and teaching about them, but what I wanted to do was be the one writing! I'd never had the audacity to regard myself in such a role. Authors were other people.

The thought pulled me out of bed and into the kitchen of my California home where I could stew about it over a cup of tea. Why didn't I study English literature or go after an MFA? Then that angst turned to blame as it occurred to me how deeply my choices had been affected by cultural expectations. Prejudice, feminism, chauvinism—the myriad of -isms that keep people "in order." Girls, in my era, became secretaries, nurses, teachers, and mothers. The daring ones became flight attendants.

It became clear to me that night, as I sat in the dark at the kitchen table with my tea and a slice of moonlight for company, that I had lived my life within human cultural definition, obediently stuffing myself into a man-made mold. Most of me fit, but cultural mores don't necessarily address the spirit. The spiritual part of me hung over the edges of the mold like excess dough around a cookie cutter. Something wasn't working.

Then, as my tea grew cold and the moonlight merged with sunlight, I relaxed and admitted that I had, indeed, felt satisfied with every decision I had made along the way at the time I had made it. I had outgrown my choices, that's all. It wasn't anybody's fault. Upon further reflection, I decided that there isn't just one thing we are called to do with our lives. That God calls us to a variety of roles along the way, each skillset building upon the last. I had been putting too much pressure on myself to figure out the "one thing" I was here to do. Maybe, there is no "one thing." Maybe, there is just the "next thing."

Sitting here in this peaceful cloister I imagined myself returning home with a new plan. The challenge at midlife would be rearranging the pieces of my life, and the effort it would take to do this "next thing" when

I figure out what it is. When one person in a family decides to make a major life shift, it affects everyone, and not always in the most convenient ways. Would all the upset it takes to change and follow a dream or calling be worth it? Worth upsetting the rhythm of a household? Worth pulling that stone block from the arch?

Sometimes it seems like an impossible choice, but I think God and I could handle it.

I placed my camera in its case and headed back through the arches to the primo chiostro as I wanted to visit the Pazzi Chapel before I left. Also designed by the great, Filippo Brunelleschi, it is widely known for its perfect acoustics.

While the overwhelming size of the basilica next door had stirred me, filling me with an energy that inspired and pushed me deeper into myself, this small space was calming. The size of a large gazebo, its geometric symmetry, white stucco walls, and light-gray stone pilasters insisted that its visitors stop and take a long, slow cleansing breath. A tiny chapel of human scale, it soothed and mollified.

Empty, I stood in the middle and slowly turned to absorb all of the detail: the columns, pilasters, arches, and vaults, the blue glazed terra-cotta roundels just below the ceiling. It was so tranquil and serene that the thought occurred to me that I could lock the door and sit for a while if I were so bold.

The last time I was here, I heard a choir singing *Ave Maria* while I was studying illuminated hymnals in one of the side rooms of the basilica. The sound was so pure and sweet that I had no choice but to find its source, though, at the time, I didn't know where I was headed.

The voices lured me out of the basilica, down the stone steps, and through the open doors of this chapel. Standing in the center, back-to-back with their eyes closed, were four twenty-something friends singing in harmony. I remember shrinking into a corner in wide-eyed wonder, absorbing the angelic tones through every pore as the music washed over me. The walls seemed to inhale the notes and then exhale them in gentle, rolling echoes. It was one of those exquisite moments where music lifted me on wings and set me free.

When they had finished, they opened their eyes and we stood staring at each other as my feet settled back onto the ground. One of them smiled at me and said, "This chapel is known for its perfect acoustics. We traveled a long way to sing that song." I told them that I guessed I had traveled some forty-odd years to hear it and asked if they would please sing another.

They looked at each other and shook their heads. A young man with a tattoo of a base clef peeking from beneath a rumpled shirt collar responded as they gathered their bags. "You can only do that once," he said. Then they were off, leaving me with a thirst for that extraordinary sound. I'd had a feeling that thirst would never again be quenched quite like that, and it hasn't so far.

It is well known in my family that I have the singing voice of a drowning cat. But here, standing with that memory, I felt the urge to give it a go. I peeked out the door and saw that the courtyard was still empty. No one would hear me. I stood for a good five minutes gathering the nerve to sing something. In the end, I pursed my lips and let out a gentle whistle. Echoes answered in dulcet, honeyed tones, so I whistled an entire tune. Instead of enjoying it, I felt like the child I used to be, unsure of my voice in a family of men. The child who was afraid to sing.

It was so stupid. What was I worried about? Why did I care so much? If I couldn't handle this tiny risk, how did I think I was going to "seize the day" going forward? One more peek out the door to make sure I was still alone, and then I did it, I sang (quietly, almost a whisper) a verse from a hymn from my childhood that always conjures the memory of my family of eight lining a pew at mass, my father's booming voice leading us in song.

Hear, O Lord, the sound of my call
Hear, O Lord, and have mercy

My soul is longing for the glory of You
So hear, O Lord, and answer me.

The walls didn't inhale or exhale my notes in rolling echoes, but it was beautiful—to me.

I felt a shift. I guess I had been waiting some forty-odd years to do that.

Texts from Home: Part 3

Matthew: Mom. Alert, alert!! Dad bought a new chandelier for the dining room!

 Me: What?!

 Matthew: I know!

 Me: I thought we discussed your urging him not to make any decorating decisions without me.

 Matthew: I tried.

 Me: How does it look?

 Matthew: Sort of . . . um . . . interesting.

 Me: Shoot.

 Matthew: :) I have the receipt in my desk drawer.

 Me: Good thinking.

 Matthew: Can I take some money from your secret stash in the back of your closet for the movies?

Me: No.

Matthew: But you have thirty-five dollars in there.

Me: It's supposed to be secret. Fine, you can have twenty. Stop snooping. Love you.

Matthew: Love you too.

CHAPTER 11

A Time to Let Go - Part 2

An earnest waiter, impeccable in a bright-red jacket, led
me to a table at the historic Caffè Le Giubbe Rosse (the
Red Jackets Café). Located on the Piazza della Repubblica, Florence's main square, it is an age-old haunt of
writers. I was meeting the kids in this part of town
tonight, so I decided to splurge on dinner.

In the early 1900s, Le Giubbe Rosse was the
meeting place of the literary elite. The café boasted
newspapers and magazines from all over the world and
soon became home to the literati of the day. It evolved
into an unofficial political think tank, and those who
founded the Italian futurist movement gathered here to
discuss what the future might hold for Italy. The
important avant-garde journals Solaria and Lacerba

were birthed in these rooms. Journalists, writers, and painters sipped grappa here and argued late into the night, cigarette smoke swirling and clawing at the dim bulbs hanging over their heads.

It was a busy evening, most of the tables filled with locals and tourists alike. The clink of silverware and murmur of conversation were comforting. I wondered if people were discussing new ideas or rehashing old ones. Perhaps a little of both.

I scooted the high-backed wooden chairs close to the table, covered in red linen, and settled in for the evening. While I waited for Katie and her friends, I scanned the walls, filled with artwork, sketches, framed newspaper articles, photos, and memorabilia. A rack of books was propped against a wall. The waiter handed me a menu and, when he saw me glancing at the books, explained that the café still hosted literary meetings once a week. There is something holy and inspiring about sitting in a room with such a history of important conversation. It worries me that our kids are limiting their conversations to text messages and photos. I want them to experience the power of honest and exploratory discourse. To know that their deep thoughts are worth discussing.

I turned to see Katie and Will, with broad smiles and flushed cheeks, striding toward me. Katie wore a sunny yellow wool coat that accented her blonde hair, and Will, with a proprietary hand on her back, was sure and handsome in a navy jacket and striped gray scarf furled around his neck.

"Hey, Mom." Katie said as the three of us exchanged hugs and hellos.

"Where's Laura?" I asked. "Is she okay?" I had yet to set eyes on Katie's roommate and dear friend. Motherly instincts on alert, I wanted visual contact before I left Florence to make sure she was fine.

"She sends her love," Katie answered. "She was tired and decided to grab a quick bite with our other roommates and go to bed early."

"Jet lag," added Will. "It comes in waves."

"Well, I'm glad you made it," I said as I passed them the menus. "I'm dying to hear about everything." Katie opened hers while Will looked around.

"So, this place is famous?" said Will as his eyes roamed the old photographs overhead.

"I'm hoping the magic rubs off on me," I laughed.

"Katie tells me you're here on business?"

I exchanged knowing looks with Katie and said, "What were the chances. Right?"

"Seriously," he replied.

We ordered a bottle of Chianti and a "Redcoat," the restaurant's name for its bistecca alla Fiorentia, to split three ways. A traditional Florentine meal, this was a large, very rare, T-bone steak cooked over charcoal. The waiter tried to persuade us to get one each, but I had a feeling we'd have plenty.

As we sipped red wine, I learned all that had transpired since their arrival. Katie would start a story, and Will would finish it. They were scared and happy and exhausted and confused, and, clearly, in love.

"Even our way here tonight was filled with surprises!" Katie continued her stories one after the next with barely a breath in between. "First, we walked by this tiny ambulance the size of a minivan. We could see the person inside on the stretcher moving around with an IV stuck in his arm. The back doors were wide open, and people were walking by looking inside like it was no big deal. No one seemed concerned in the least."

"The two medics were leaning against the side smoking a cigarette," added Will.

"We were like, 'Hello, people! A quick run to the hospital might be in order!'" Katie laughed and continued in a dramatic voice, "And then . . . we passed this shop that had a huge life-sized Pinocchio sitting on a bench out front."

"Katie made me take about twenty photos of her sitting next to him. I swear we have every possible angle," said Will as he pulled a tiny camera from his pocket and showed us a photo of Katie with Pinocchio's arm draped over her shoulder like they were old chums.

"Come on, it was Pinocchio, for goodness' sake. It's not every day you get to walk down the streets where Pinocchio was written!"

As they continued with tales of Pinocchio, I remembered the scene in *Father of the Bride* when

Steve Martin's daughter is telling him that she met the love of her life in Rome and was engaged to be married. Steve Martin turns and sees her not as a young woman in love, but as the freckled-faced seven-year-old in pigtails that she used to be. I looked at Katie and Will and saw two little kids in a reading group discussing their storybook in a second-grade classroom.

I am always aware that time is passing, but, like tonight, there are lucid moments when I stop and can't believe that it is real. This girl of mine was no longer a girl. I was not sure, however, what to call her. When does adolescence end and adulthood begin? Certainly, she was past adolescence, but she was not yet an adult, not fully. Wasn't it just yesterday morning that she was afraid she couldn't handle this?

A young adult? No, they called her that in eighth grade. New adult? Emerging adult? I was now noticing this phrase as the new lingo bantered about. Emerging from the home, I guess. No, I thought, as I reached for the bread basket. We needed a new term here. The transition to adulthood is subjective and varying. Who can say with finality the precise moment that bridge is crossed?

I knew that my being here was delaying that process for Katie a tad, but, frankly, I didn't care. There is a fine line to be drawn between help and hindrance. As much as it is a process for the child, it is a process for the parent as well. Birds may ruthlessly push their babies from the nest when it is time to fly, but the babies fly *away*.

How do you birth children, hold them in your arms and on your hip for months, nurse them through illness, teach them to read, watch them grow wide-eyed with wonder at the sight of the ocean, giggle with them under low-hanging blankets of a homemade fort in the living room, support them through years of study and schoolyard politics—and then think that you can just push them out the door and close it? Even Mary followed Jesus around, and no one complained about that.

I remember my friend Debbie urging me to get rid of Katie's midnight curfew when she was in high school. She told me that I had to "let Katie practice being an adult." I knew she was right, but I couldn't do it. Not with teenage drinking and driving and sex.

"That will never go away," Debbie had said. "She'll never grow up if you don't let her."

"She can grow up when she's older," I'd replied.

All along I knew Katie needed opportunities to make her own choices and practice figuring out how to handle the ones that didn't work out. I took chances, let her go, and she learned more than a few important things about what it took to be successful in the world, but, maybe, she would have learned a lot more had I been able to unlock the dead bolts on our doors.

I took another gulp of Chianti and sighed inwardly.

From the looks of her right now, it didn't appear that I had ruined her.

I heard someone say, once, that we spend our entire life separating from our children. Honestly? I don't think we ever do, and I'm not sure why we feel like we have to. The bond between parent and child never wanes. Sure, there is a loosening of the strings. Enough play for the kite to soar and climb and circle the globe. However, I don't know a single parent who lets go entirely. Who wants to watch their beautiful kite soar away? Shoestrings to apron strings to kite strings to heartstrings. The visible to the invisible but forever attached.

Schools of thought change, society shifts, recessions come and go. Children learn and grow and eventually find their way, and, in the process, we keep the entire psychology and self-help industry afloat with our constant questioning. Some kids run full throttle, their nature a ball of forward-rolling energy. Others, however, don't. Sometimes the moment the bridge into adulthood is crossed is the moment the parent decides to walk them across and then kiss them good-bye. But I will never fault the parent that takes a year or two longer to do that. The time that a parent and child share on that bridge is sacred, and it's not easy to take our child's now-not-so-tiny hand and place it in God's. Maybe, we should call this time *bridging*. I like that. It's a forgiving term. There's room on a bridge for all sorts of people and all sorts of situations. Since every bridge has an end point, the child eventually moves to a new landscape, ready or not.

Our waiter appeared with a large wooden cutting board on which was a handful of salad greens and the largest slab of beef I had ever seen. Across the corner of the board, in brown sauce, were the words Giubbe Rosse in perfect script.

"Thank you! We'll take another bottle of that Chianti," I said as the waiter helped us cut portions and serve them.

"Si, si. With pleasure." He bowed deeply, to our collective amusement.

As we left the restaurant, we agreed to meet again the next night, so I could spend time with Laura before I left for Genoa. Outside, the piazza was alive with the music and dancing of local peddlers and gypsies. The merrily lit antique wooden carousel of the Picci family was spinning nearby, each horse's saddle filled with a happy child, parents filling the spaces between the horses, making sure their little ones didn't fall as they rode to the accompaniment of accordion music.

A three-quarter moon floated in and out of a threatening cloud bank, and the smell of rain was in the air. We remarked about how a January night on the Piazza della Repubblica was so much more exciting than a January night at home. In the future, every such night I sat bored in front of the TV, I would remember that this was happening across the world. That I could be standing here instead of flipping through channels if I wanted.

After a group hug, I headed across the piazza toward my hotel near the Duomo, and Katie and Will headed toward their new apartments. As happy as I was, there was that ache again that I needed to shoo away. Our family was changing, and that was that. I had to let go. I inhaled deeply to arrest the sad feelings and replace them with positive thoughts.

"Not a bad day, was it?" I said aloud to myself with forced cheerfulness. "And a great night too."

I turned for one last look, and, silhouetted against the lights of the carousel and the glow of the buildings behind them, Katie and Will were slow-dancing, foreheads together, like they were the only two people that mattered. As it should be.

CHAPTER 12

So This is Peace

Having the entire day to myself—Katie would be in classes—I decided to treat it like a gift. I would unwrap it slowly and be surprised by the contents inside. It's my favorite way to journey. The less expectation I put on a day, the more I am enchanted by the random joys inherent in being present in each moment. My sense of wonder, lulled to sleep by the day-to-day rush of life back home, awakens and stretches its arms.

Not to say that I haven't had some horrible travel days, where I am stranded or pushed around by strangers. Gypsies that try (or succeed) in stealing my purse or backpack. I've had plenty of challenges on the road, but a sense of humor, a deep breath, a good meal, and a glass of wine can get me through almost anything.

The waiter at the café this morning had insisted, with flailing arms and widened blue eyes, that I climb to the Piazzale Michelangelo on the south side of the Arno River. Anything that evoked such emotion had to be worth the hike, so, after a cappuccino and a freshly baked cornetto (a croissant-like pastry filled with apricot jam), I made my way toward the river. I had never been south of the Arno, so today I would explore new territory.

Though it was a chilly morning, street artists already lined a few of the streets and alleyways. Sauntering past them, I browsed the various canvases, exchanging pleasantries as I examined the various ink drawings and watercolors of famous landmarks around town. One woman walked boldly to me and pressed a small stack of postcard-sized paintings against my arm.

"Beautiful colors," I said to her, gently pushing them back into her manicured hands. "I'll think about it."

Her brown eyes clouded as a "harrumph" escaped pursed coral lips. Then she looked through me like I wasn't standing there letting me know that I was in her way, blocking another sale or the hope of one. Her quick dismissal of me only clarified what I could already see. Her art wasn't real—the colors too vivid, the lines too precise. She didn't even try to hide the stencils that spilled from the leather tote bag that sank into the cobblestones like caramel melting in the sun.

She didn't birth these creations; she spit them out. It was a business, plain and simple. Certainly not a crime —we all have to make a living—but art should speak of your secrets, and those can't be found in a stencil.

There was a time when the artists I passed on my travels were all authentic. When the displayed pieces were unique, well loved, and worried over. The painters and sculptors were mysterious creatures to me. I imagined they barely scraped by, living day to day. Part of me would worry for them as they sat on folding chairs in patched shirts and shoes with worn laces. I would picture the same misshapen fingers and rough hands cutting a loaf of bread for dinner at the end of a long day, in a studio apartment with sloping floors that creaked. The other part of me, though, always noted their contented eyes, crinkled with lines above half-moon smiles.

When I bought something, it was because I wanted to take a piece of the artist home. A piece that they had decided was ripe for the picking. Fruit of their labors that had come into season. Those were the pieces that sang.

Most of the original artwork that we have hanging on the walls of our home has come from street artists. The imperfect, accessible quality draws me to them. Deepens my appreciation of the complexities of the human spirit. They brighten my day when I happen to glance at one. I am transported back to the moment that I crossed paths with the artist, perhaps under an olive tree beside the dirt path on the Cinque Terre, near a line of horse-drawn carriages on a frigid Sunday in Salzburg, in a restaurant by the sea in the tiny fishing village of Camogli. I can recall the conversation, the tone of the voice, the artist's happy promise that his or her piece would forever bring me joy. What I bought wasn't paint and paper; it was connection to the divine in them.

I meandered along a shadowy corridor near the Palazzo Vecchio, past other fake artists and hawkers of imitation Gucci bags and Rolex watches. I was getting disgusted with the whole scene when I saw an empty wooden easel with a stack of canvases leaning against its spindly legs. The colors called to me first. Sophisticated, layered pigments with an energy that beckoned.

Glancing around, I didn't see anyone. No one guarding these canvases with paint-free hands, no one looking through me. I sauntered over and studied a depiction of a bicycle leaning against a graffitied wall near a darkened entryway; the bike's wheels reflected in puddles on a street that glistened with rain. Two wheels waiting to turn. Who owned this bike? Where would it go next? Would someone ride it through a maze of streets in search of a lost love? Through a thawing countryside of early spring? Why this alley? Who lived here?

A burly man with ruddy skin and frown lines like parentheses lumbered toward me in a rumpled olive overcoat, lugging a three-legged stool and two splintery vegetable crates. If I had met him in a bar, I would have given him a wide berth, but because his soul was on parade, I wanted to know him.

"Is this your bike?" I asked.

"Just one I saw," he replied as he arranged the crates side by side, "but I saw it every day. Only at certain times."

"What about this green door?" I asked, pointing to another piece.

"My mother's. She can barely open it now. Arthritis." He continued matter-of-factly with his setup. I was merely a passerby to him, but he didn't make me feel like an intruder.

"This blue door, here." I pointed to another canvas. "This one is open. There are shadows." He turned patiently, like a parent who finally gives attention to a pestering child and regarded me with hazel eyes that saw through me in a different way. "Of course, there are shadows. Where else would we hide our truths?" he said. Crinkled smile lines appeared as he squinted at me. I felt something pass between us. A knowing.

"I guess." I gulped. "I like the shade of blue, like a morning glory. That's what drew me."

"Are you sure?" he said.

"Perhaps the shadow made me wonder what was inside," I pondered.

He selected a painting from his pile and set it on the easel. It burned with bold strokes of

red. Painted from an interesting angle, it depicted

the top half of a red cafe door and the shuttered apartment window above it. A flower box beneath the window overflowed with tiny pink blooms, and the words "art," "Firenze," and "dello studio" were etched in the wall.

"Is this your studio? Your home?" I asked as I held it up to the sunlight. He straightened in a way that belied an aching back and raked thick fingers through shaggy blond hair. For an instant I saw him as he must have looked as a young man, swarthy and handsome.

"That is where I live," he said with a slight grin and then added, "in my mind." I pictured him, all of a sudden, breaking bread with bent fingers in a shadowy flat with a slanted floor that creaked.

"Me too." We shared a laugh, knowing that we all have dreams. "Your English is good," I added.

"My mother is American," he said.

"Can I take a photo of these?" I assumed he would say no. No one ever lets you do that. "Why not," he said.

"Really?"

"Sure." He wasn't the least bit concerned. I could take this photo and have it printed on

canvas a world away. He knew it, and he didn't care. But I would care. Sure, it would be charming in the space on the wall near my kitchen sink, but it wouldn't just remind me of our meeting; it would remind me of the fact that I did not buy a piece of his soul that day. The truth was that I didn't have money to spend on his paintings, though I would have had I been able. As I snapped photo after photo, I felt like a big cheapskate, but I kept going because I wasn't ready to leave. The clicking of the lens shutter filling the space between us was helping me stall.

There was something tranquil, grounding, and calming about this artist. An ordinary guy doing what he loved. If you wanted to buy a painting, that was fine. If you didn't, that was fine too. I am inspired by the people among us who quietly go about their art and create beauty just for the sake of it. They bring serenity to their little patch of world.

Suddenly I realized that this scene was "peace in action" right here in front of me. I envisioned all of the world's citizens spending their time and energy creating whatever artful desire God gifted to them at birth. How different, how peaceful, the world would be if we all brought serenity to our little patch of world. Why aren't we teaching that in schools?

Another woman paused to admire his work and exchange pleasantries. I listened as she asked questions about the same pieces, noticing that her questions differed from mine though equally revealing. Art born of authentic creative impulse is a pathway inward for the seeker. She chose a piece, and he wrapped it in plain brown paper.

I was jealous in a way. He was already doing what most of us are afraid to do. Claim our art, wholly. Practice it, unapologetically, without a care about proving a thing to anyone. As I snapped photo after photo of my street artist's paintings, I found myself back at the door with the shadows. Did I have the courage to come out of the shadows? Would I rededicate my life to my passion and start another book, or not? Why was I not doing my best to bring peace to my little corner of the world? I was having trouble deciding whether to make writing a permanent career choice or keep it safely to the side as my successful hobby. There's a lower bar of expectation for hobbies. I was afraid that I didn't have what it takes to compete on a national stage of writers with long lists of titles and awards.

As Thomas Aquinas reminds us, we have to believe in ourselves first. "We can't have full knowledge all at once. We must start by believing, then afterwards we may be led on to master the evidence for ourselves."

How much is being genuine worth? Would it be worth choosing a life that might result in patched shirts and worn shoelaces? Is it more important to shine or to illuminate others? Maybe it's a little bit of both.

"Good luck today," I said to the artist as I put my camera back into its case. I had reached the time limit for being a casual observer, and it would have been awkward for me to stay.

"You too," he replied as I waved and wandered off.

Looking to the sky, I made a vow: I wouldn't make any more excuses as to why I am

wasting my gifts. With renewed effort and ingenuity, I would try again to marry my passion for writing with business, knowing that doing so wouldn't be easy.

Like St. Thomas said, I had to begin by believing. It would be work, but it would be joyful, heart-filled work.

When I feel tired or discouraged, and I know those days will come, I will remember this street artist, my unlikely hero. I will remember his kindness, his peaceful countenance, and his wisdom. How we are drawn to the shadows, which just may hold the true self that is hiding from the sun.

I will remind myself that genuine is always worth it.

CHAPTER 13

Seeking New Perspectives

Continuing on, I joined the throng of sightseers that jostled its way down the Lungarno delle Grazie, the street that borders the Arno River. The crowd's tempo pushed me forward, and absorbing its energy, I quickened my pace, relishing the happy mayhem of the city: a susurrus of languages, zooming taxis, the roar of Vespas, the hawking of street vendors, the clink of coins tossed into a beggar's wooden bowl. A sweat-stained horse the color of India ink strained against his worn leather harness and clomped beside me, tugging a white buggy with large wheels that squeaked as they wobbled over the cobblestone.

Every city sings its own song. Some cities are dignified and self-possessed, humming in hushed tones.

Others croon melodies that sashay and shimmy with a sexual energy, and some places pulse with fragmented and jumbled harmonies. A few try to hide their sorrowful laments beneath monuments, but I am not easily fooled. Human misery, shame, and remorse quietly wail in a way one might mistake as the soft moan of wind through the branches of trees. The song of Florence? I had yet to define it as there were so many notes, chords, and rhythms. I would need more time.

Pleasantly hypnotized by the cacophony, I made my way slowly. The tolling of bells, the call of a coxswain to his rowers in a quad scull on the river below, the coo of pigeons searching for crumbs, and the whistling and wheezing of accordion music from a narrow alley. Wallowing in joy, I became aware of a constant click of cameras that made me turn to see if I was missing something. There, several hundred yards away was the Ponte Vecchio, Florence's most famous bridge, with its three arches connecting the south bank of the Arno River to the north.

Scores of admirers stood along the bank staring at it and attempting to capture it on camera or on canvas. The Ponte Vecchio, or "Old Bridge," is the only surviving bridge from medieval times. All the others were destroyed by the Germans during World War II as they retreated from North Africa into Italy and back to Germany while the Allies made their way north. The Ponte Vecchio links the glory days of Italy to the present.

I snapped a few photos, though I had a slew of them already at home. Then I did something that surprised me. I quietly apologized to historians worldwide, gave a nod of resignation to the photographers on my left and right, and deleted the images. The Old Bridge was glorious and artistically sublime, especially when the sun sank behind it, setting it ablaze. Intellectually I understood its magnificence, but emotionally it didn't move me. I don't know why.

In my new seeking mode, I was practicing authenticity, even in the little things. I have become tired of looking at the same items and objects everyone else is looking at, just because I am expected to. Unless it stirs my soul, I don't have the time left to fake it, or the room for its image on my camera. I respect the greatness of the Ponte Vecchio, but I will never love it.

I turned eastward and continued a forward gait. The crowd thinned as I ventured beyond the historic city center. The late afternoon sun had begun to sag, and wisps of white clouds snagged on the hazy surface of the sky. I crossed another bridge to the south shore and headed up the winding hill of San Miniato, following the signs for the Piazzale Michelangelo.

I picked my way through crooked side streets to a steep series of wide stone stairs bordered on the right side by spreading maples and on the left by a tall stone wall. Up I went, loosening my jacket and unfurling my scarf as I began to perspire. I ascended, step after step, my heart thumping against my ribs. Street noises softened. The cries of children and a distant police siren gave way to the tranquilizing sights and sounds of nature rustling and swaying about me. Two flies buzzed past my head, and a burly black cat creeping through ferns regarded me with eyes the color of pollen. A twig cracked beneath its paws.

Stopping to catch my breath, I peered through the stand of trees. Dappled sunlight upon tangled under-brush played tricks with my eyes. A lazy breeze shuffled through branches already budding in January. One hundred fifty-nine steps so far—not that I was counting.

As I continued, I thought about my innate desire to climb. Perhaps it was the sensation of seeking that satisfied, or the appreciation that it takes effort to be given a new perspective. Perhaps it was knowing that I was as physically close to the sky as I could be at that moment.

At the top of the stairs, I paused, took a deep breath, and turned left. Before me spread the Piazzale Michelangelo, an expansive square designed by archi-tect Giuseppe Poggi and dedicated to Michelangelo in 1869. Walking toward it I saw a bronze replica of Michelangelo's David, standing proudly on a raised pedestal in the center, sling over his shoulder and stone in hand, watching over the city. My mouth fell open, and my eyes widened into the same incredulous expression that the waiter had treated me to that morn-ing. Like a child who had turned a corner to lay her eyes upon the ocean for the first time, I found myself dumbfounded. It was a lot to take in at once.

Now this was a sight that moved me, that made me want to take my camera and click away. The irony of it was that I knew that these photographs would prove flat. They wouldn't hold the depth of feeling nor the rush of amazement when I scrolled through them on my computer screen during a coffee break, months from now, or even if I printed them out.

Gazing at the panoramic view of Florence and the surrounding countryside, I stood transfixed. Compared to the view from the top of the Duomo, the energy and scope here was far more expansive: a maze of red roofs, cream-colored buildings, and distant mountains; jagged and worn stone walls from another era snaking through the Tuscan hills; cypress trees standing shoulder to shoulder on the horizon; a hazy mist rising from the earth to meet the sky; the river golden with the reflective glow of the sinking sun.

To the west down the Arno stood the three bridges: the Ponte Vecchio, the Ponte Santa Trinita, and the Ponte alla Carraia. To the northwest, the clock tower from the Palazzo Vecchio commanded respect and the colossal dome of the Duomo rose above the skyline. To the north, the white facade of Santa Croce reflected the sun, and the great synagogue of Florence, the Tempio Israelitico, stood steadfast and proud. Farther northeast, the newer parts of the city spread toward the hills, and continuing upriver to the east, the

Arno flowed toward the Ponte di San Niccolò and the Ponte da Verrazzano.

Tourists lined the railing on both sides of me. Lovers embraced, eyes searched the horizons, and the updraft of the wind mingled with reverent murmurs. The slow and sensual strum of a guitar caught my attention, and I ventured to the edge of the piazza to a set of stone stairs—stadium seating that covered the hillside. It was crowded with people of all ages and nationalities. A makeshift stage was set at the far end, where a young musician in an orange sweater, her hair tucked under a striped kerchief, sang, in an Italian accent, a soulful "Killing Me Softly with His Song."

I scooted behind a group of crooning students who swayed in time, drawn to the melody and to each other. A couple about my age with backpacks and cameras sat nearby fiddling with maps and gently teasing each other. A young family, two children snuggled on their parents' laps, snacked on peanuts and shared a Coke. All of us strangers, yet not. I didn't feel alone but part of a contented slice of the universe. I envisioned a moment in the future when I would meet someone by chance who had also been here, and we would share a knowing nod when we found that we had both sat on these steps, that we had shared this particular magic.

I gazed at the panorama for a long while, and what struck me from this vantage point was the varying scale of Florence's architecture. I was staying in a hotel, literally, next to the Duomo, the enormity of which took my breath away every time I stepped out the door. All else in the neighborhood was dwarfed in its presence. From here, however, set against the other buildings, set against the hills of Settignano and Fiesole, the grand Duomo seemed even *larger* in scale.

There was a big difference though. From this distance, from this perspective, I could see that the Duomo was merely part of a whole—a big part, but only one stop in this majestic city. If I had not followed the advice of the barista, had I stayed in the neighborhoods surrounding the Duomo, I would be missing all the beauty that stretched in every direction.

The large, difficult issues of our lives—be they divorce, illness, the death of a loved one, bankruptcy, or a myriad of others—are like the Duomo. Sometimes we stand in the shadow of its enormity for so long that we lose our frame of reference. A new perspective doesn't make our issues less large and important. It just reminds us that there is still a big, beautiful world around them, waiting to be explored. Taking time to wander doesn't mean we are ignoring our issues; it simply gives us a chance to put them in perspective. To see our trials as part of God's provenance.

Changing our perspective can change our lives. And like the climb up the mountain to get here, it's easier said than done. Our wisdom lies in the accepting that this may just be what our personal skyline looks like.

I stood and turned my face to a considerable wind that had strengthened as it swirled up the hillside. The young musician in the orange sweater began to sing "Where is the Love" another Roberta Flack song. Clearly a '70s groove going on here, songs that comprised the backdrop of my youth. The crowd collectively swayed with the beat of the music, even the young couples who were not alive when Roberta Flack and Donny Hathaway recorded it, mouthed the words.

Perspectives may change, but some things are timeless: this song, this view, this hopeful feeling.

Texts from Home: Part 4

Matthew: Hi, Mom. Tell Katie to stop texting me during class. I got in trouble today.

    Me: Can you turn off your phone during school?

    Matthew: What if you have to tell me something? What if I need to talk to you?

    Me: Good point. I'll remind her. Text her when you can. It means a lot to her to have your support.

    Matthew: I'll send her some funny YouTube videos later.

    Me: Perfect.

    Matthew: Oh, and Mrs. Cavanaugh wants to know if you'll run the school fashion show.

    Me: (What I want to say: I'd rather stick a pin in my eye.) Please tell Mrs. Cavanaugh that I appreciate her faith in my abilities, but I respectfully decline.

Tim: Hi, Honey. Fixing a few things around the house. I think you'll be surprised! Are you having a good time? How's Katie?

Me: Thanks for all of your hard work. :) You are the best. Katie is settling in. I really haven't seen her all that much. She's in class all day, and she's had a few student orientation events at night. We've had a few dinners.

Tim: So, basically, you're on vacation.

Me: Sort of. ;)

CHAPTER 14

It's a Great Life if You Don't Weaken

It was late in the afternoon, and I was about to leave Piazzale Michelangelo to hike down the hillside of Oltrarno toward the center of Florence when the tolling of church bells began, primal and alluring, marking the top of the hour. Looking for the source, I spied a sign that pointed left, upward, to the basilica of San Miniato al Monte. I checked my watch and knew that I needed to leave in order to be on time for a dinner reservation, but an opportunity to explore was at hand. Right here, right now. Chances of coming back here this week were slim, and what if my propensity to be timely and disciplined (a.k.a. dull and boring) prevented me from experiencing something significant? Who knew what lay above?

If I had learned anything from my year of living dangerously in Genoa, it was to let go of "shoulds" and follow paths that called to me. Almost without fail, a lovely or amazing discovery would reveal itself. Something important.

I figured that Katie and her friend, Laura, could entertain each other until I arrived at the restaurant, so I headed up the hill another quarter of a mile to a set of steep white, stone stairs that ascended to the church, its Romanesque facade a combination of alabaster and moss-green marble framed against a deepening indigo sky. Above the center door, gold mosaics shimmered, as if radiating a light of their own.

A few tourists stood near the curb. I could hear them wondering aloud if they should exert themselves for "just another church." They were tired—hadn't they climbed enough stairs for one day? It was clear they were unaware of the gift of perspective. That the higher you rise above the fray, the sharper into focus what really matters to you will come. I didn't tell them. Who needs whining to ruin a good view?

I gritted my teeth and climbed. Take me higher, I thought to myself between breaths. Enchant me. Soon I was standing on flat land beholding an even more amazing vista of the Tuscan countryside. Gazing westward, I willed the scenery to imprint itself upon me as the sun continued melting down the back side of the sky. An elderly monk tottered by in an ivory robe cinched at the waist by a brown rope, his shadow trailing behind him. He seemed to float, an angel with a cane.

From this vantage point I saw that the church was only one portion of a compound that included an ancient monastery. I decided that I could peek inside the church after dark, but I wanted to walk the grounds as the sun set. To my left was a brick archway and a path that led around the side of the property. I headed through it expecting to see gardens and a shrine or two. What I did not expect was the entrance to the cemetery to end all cemeteries. Nothing like walking into a graveyard to dampen a fine mood.

I did not climb this hillside to work through my thoughts of death, but here I was standing, literally, in the midst of it. Again, my teacher had appeared, deftly luring me here to press my nose to my greatest fear. Because I have learned that the only way to deal with pain is to walk right through it, I accepted the invitation to explore my feelings.

I took a centering breath and moved forward. Took the step I had been avoiding. I began by wandering slowly, carefully treading around the maze of tombs. The cemetery was crowded with headstones and sculptures, carvings of cherubs and crosses and children. Obelisks and columns balanced on pedestals; full-scale angels guarded tombs while weeping and praying. Sculptures of grieving mothers pleaded, reached, and wailed. A life-sized muscled warrior lay, face down in surrender across one grave, clutching a victory torch, extinguished. The bust of a dashing gentleman in a top hat, a cloaked woman crying on the steps of a mausoleum, strewn with silk lilies and ceramic roses. Hanging lamps, brassy and rusted, were lit with tiny electric bulbs that grew bright as the sunlight faded.

This was not just any old graveyard; this was a prayer. A mesmerizing tribute to life, brilliant and brimming with sentiment. I have long understood that Italians are a passionate people. Their joie de vivre had lifted me from the darkest point of my life, but I did not know that they were also passionate about death. This was an outdoor museum of sepulchral artwork at its finest, the artistic rendering of the searing emotions that mark our lives.

A maroon jacket zigzagging slowly at the far end of the property caught my eye. From this distance I could see it was a man, aged and crooked, carrying a brown paper bag. He bent for a moment, picked something off the ground, and placed it in his bag.

I drifted, studied, photographed, and in so doing began to get a sense of those buried here and those they left behind—variations of grays and whites in a dance of days gone by. Curiously, I didn't feel an absence of color. I felt all of them, every shade. I imagined blue and pink baby blankets and the sweet yellow crinoline of a preteen beauty. I glimpsed navy uniforms with gold buttons, and black boots with worn heels and tattered laces. Around a corner a sensible brown dress curtsied, boasting a collar of fine lace, and a trio of smoky pin-striped suits pressed with straight seams gathered to discuss the news of the day. I stared into framed photos fixed above chiseled names, loved ones with serious eyes and smiles edged in mystery. I was walking through a history book.

The wind rushed through the branches of the cypresses that stood guard across the rear of the property, speaking to me in the whispers of the dead. They were beautiful whispers, like the fragrance of orange blossoms. They said things like: I have been loved. I was a hero to someone. I mattered. I have lived a life that deserves a headstone that cries for eternity.

A few weeks ago, I was pedaling my bike along a path near a cemetery in Arizona. I had stopped for a moment to tie a shoelace that had come undone, and I noticed a young woman on a bench with her head bent in prayer. I wondered who she was visiting, for whom she was aching. The cemetery, from my vantage point, was a green field with flat stones like shoe boxes lined in straight rows. It was neat, orderly, and sterile. It offended me, the way it erased lives. I want to mark the earth when I die. I don't want to disappear, politely, into a plot that bows to a lawn mower.

These last few years I have become increasingly beset with the subject of death. I have already begun to mourn the passing of my parents, my husband, my siblings and friends—and they are as alive as I am. Every day there is a moment when I tell myself that I now have one less opportunity to call my mother or my father, feel my husband's arms around me, hear my brothers' voices, exchange sweet sarcasm and laughter with a friend. Part of me wants to camp out in their guest rooms just to stare at them, to breathe in their essence.

Some days I call my parents, and while talking about things like grocery lists and brands of coffee, my heart screams "Don't die!" so loudly that I cover the mouthpiece, so they can't hear it. Another part of me wants to perish first so I don't have to bear the grief. I have borne all sorts of things in my life, but I honestly don't believe that I have the emotional strength for final good-byes. I just don't. I fear them with all of my being.

I remember reading one time that a person should be buried in a place where the earth knows them. That sentence made my mouth go dry, my stomach clench into a mass of granite. I didn't have a place that knew me. I was a rolling stone, though I'd never wanted to roll in the first place. Sure, my childhood in New Jersey was long and steady, but my married life had taken me across the nation and overseas. My hometown cradled me for eighteen years, but that world had dissipated decades ago into a mist of remember whens. My soul was homeless. I wondered if I should include a clause in my will that provided for a moving van to pick up my casket and move it every three years.

I stopped for a moment to catch my breath, looking to the horizon to steady myself. The shadows were lengthening, and, all of a sudden, eternity didn't look so far away. Still, I felt like an intruder. A show-off. Like I was parading my pumping heart, flaunting my warm skin. I stepped more carefully and respectfully through the graveyard, translating the inscriptions: Rest in peace, Sleeping with the angels, Sadly missed, In loving remembrance, In memory of, Eternally loved.

I think that headstones are only half-inscribed. One side should be a historical reference with a name and dates that communicate a life span, but the other should be the real tribute. Because aren't the details the true measure of a life? Beloved father says one thing, but Dad, I can't live without your corny jokes and the sound of your footsteps upon that old linoleum you refused to update says quite another. Treasured mother is fine enough, but Mom, whose laughing eyes will I search for over a crowded room when someone makes a social gaffe or dresses inappropriately? captures so much more.

Two summers ago, my mother and I took a trip to Troy, New York, to attend a family celebration. My mother spent her childhood in the nearby small suburb of Watervliet. As children, we used to love to make the three-hour drive there from New Jersey, so she could take us on the grand tour of her youth. We'd drive by the brick house on Second Avenue where her grandmother had lived, and the second-story flat where she'd spent her early years. We'd pass the Catholic high school where she was once crowned prom queen, and the nursing school she attended which was down the street from Rensselaer Polytechnic Institute, where she met my dad.

She'd show us the train tracks where the tramps huddled around fires near the Erie Canal and retell the story of the notorious George Van Auken, the hobo she always said we'd end up like if we didn't work hard in school. Then we'd pay tribute to the house where Frances, her best friend and partner in crime, had lived. We'd end the tour by ordering foot-longs at the hot-dog stand known for the best chili dogs on the planet.

During those trips, my mother would always make a point to drive us to the pastoral cemetery where my grandparents, Hester and Millard, were buried. We'd file out of our white station wagon and make an afternoon of it, imagining the life stories associated with the headstones we passed as we clambered up the hill searching for the two inscriptions that would call us to silence and remembrance.

That particular morning two years ago, after coffee, since we had a few hours before the family event was to start, my mother and I set off on our usual pilgrimage. We drove down Route 787 toward Albany Rural Cemetery, chatting about life, but as we exited the highway my mother unexpectedly pulled to the side of the ramp and said, "Let's not go."

"What?" I said, my eyes blinking in disbelief. "Of course, we have to go. It might be years before we get back to the East Coast."

"Grandma wouldn't mind," she said, her hands gripping the steering wheel.

"I know, but . . . it's tradition." What was going on here?

"She's not actually there, you know."

"Mom, we can't be this close and turn around." I needed to go. I loved my grandparents, and if I lived closer, I would make this journey often. It was one of those cemeteries that would be a hit in Hollywood. Mighty oaks and maples, old stone markers with names half-worn, hills and wandering paths. They weren't tombstones to me; they were touchstones. I needed to touch them.

Looking back now, I wondered if my insistence had been wrong, if I was pushing something that was too painful. Maybe it wasn't about the sadness of her parents being gone, but the fear of her own mortality. There are some things that you just don't discuss with your parents when you are driving toward a cemetery. We turned right on Cemetery Avenue and drove through the iron gates. The property was considerable, and I could never remember where to turn, but my mother always knew the exact spot to park the car. I don't think you ever forget the place where your parents are buried.

We climbed a slope through unkempt grass and scanned the headstones. Irish names, all of them, like Doyle, MacDermott, O'Callahan, Sweeney, and

O'Leary. I heard the soft sigh of heartache, a heavy still-ness, a sacred hush.

"It's over there." My mother pointed as she walked ahead. I stopped as I passed other grave sites and righted a few flower pots that had fallen sideways. As I anchored the pots as best I could, I saw Mom pause in a way that I knew she had found them. Her hesitant posture held a weight that only those who grieve would fully comprehend. I wanted to give her some privacy, so I busied myself arranging a Mrs. Maguire's faded yellow silk snapdragons that had been scattered by the wind.

Then, from my kneeling position, I spied a splotch of bright red a few feet away. I reached for it and found a silk poppy, its black-button center tangled in the grass. I looked around for its source but could see no other vases toppled. Then I stood and saw another poppy a few yards ahead, and then two more flat against the base of my grandmother's headstone. I gath-ered them, incredulously, like Hansel and Gretel finding the trail of pebbles that lead them home.

I held out my cupped hands to show my mother. "Look," I said, both of our eyes glistening with tears. The red poppies said everything we could not. "I guess she is here after all."

I had chosen the red poppy as my symbol after publishing my first book, *Halfway to Each Other*, because in one of the chapters I spoke about my grand-mother and the hat she wore every Easter. We had thought it exquisite and daring, covered in red silk poppies that bloomed above her silver curls. A hat that had turned her into a fashion statement with an exclamation point.

I searched the hillside and peered into the branches of the towering trees, expecting to see her blue eyes and sweet smile. And I was sure that I caught a drift of the pungent scent of tobacco. Good old Gramps, I could still smell his pipe twenty-five years after it went out.

My mother knelt, gently brushed away some dead leaves, and cleaned the tiny plot of land that held her parents and grandparents. We stood there for the longest time without a word. Because, really, what could words capture?

Our walk back to the car was silent but full. Part of me didn't want to leave. I've always suspected that there is some unexplained space between us and those who have passed. I wrestle with this feeling. These are the moments when I feel like I have brushed against this dimension, pierced its membrane. I find comfort in the unexplainable sense of presence, the ease of it, the lack of fear involved.

As my mother jangled her keys and unlocked the car door, our eyes met over the roof. We smiled and nodded as she recited the old family saying that we always share at the end of a conversation that has no resolution or at a moment beyond words. It's the same saying she and her mom had shared for decades when life got crazy or they simply needed to let off some steam.

"Well . . . it's a great life if you don't weaken," she said. We laughed the way we always do, and I loved her at that moment more than I could remember. I think that was the moment I began to mourn, the moment I realized that one day it would be me unlocking the car door and saying this to my own children.

I broke from my reverie when the bells of San Miniato began to toll again. I watched them swing back and forth in the old tower right above me, the clappers clanging this way and that. An hour had passed effortlessly; the light was almost gone. I made my way around the side of the church with a new understanding of why Italians cater to their dead: because in so doing, they offer the living comfort and hope. This cemetery was eerily alive, and for the first time I understood how there can be death in life and life in death.

Suddenly, the man in maroon was behind me. Unnerved, I turned to see if it was a coincidence or if he was following me. Our eyes met, and then his traveled to the camera, heavy around my neck.

"Perché le fotografie?" he demanded in a gravelly voice that was less than friendly. *Why the photographs?*

"Rispetto!" *With respect!* I quickly showed him my last shot of an exquisite sculpture of a mother and child.

He peered at the image and then back at me. There was something off about his energy, but he didn't seem dangerous. His clothes were clean, though tattered, and his paper bag was filled with litter.

"Okay?" I asked.

He nodded and pointed to a stand of trees along the rim. "Mia moglie c'è." *My wife is there.*

"Mi dispiace." *I'm sorry.*

"Il suo tempo," he said matter-of-factly. *Her time.* He held out the paper bag and smiled. "Lavori domestici. La mia casa ora." *Housework. This is my home now.*

My heart lurched. Again, a change in perspective was granting me some peace. As Teilhard de Chardin said, "We are not human beings on a spiritual journey. We are spiritual beings on a human journey." When we become aware of our spirituality and the way we connect with life's mysteries, our sorrows can sprout wings and seek flight.

I walked to the front of the church grounds to catch the edge of twilight over the layered hills. There rose a hazy darkness from the countryside, exploding into pinks and golds. I stood there and pinched myself, for the beauty of that moment was quite overwhelming.

As the horizon burned to a strip of ginger, points of light began to dot the landscape as far as I could see. Spotlights illuminated the Duomo, the Palazzo Vecchio, and other landmarks in Florence I had yet to explore. Streetlights shone along the Arno river, shops and restaurants glimmered bright welcomes, and the windows of homes busy with dinner preparations radiated. It was the glow of the living.

Night must fall for us to see and appreciate the light. In one of those glowing pinpoints, my daughter and her best friend were waiting for me, and I had a feeling that I would have more than one glass of deep-red wine. I would silently toast all of those who have gone before, but mostly I would toast to life and the joy that was all around me and within me.

I guess there are many things about death I just don't need to know the answer to right now. I have to trust that the gift of understanding will grace me when I need it. I don't know if I will lie across a loved one's tomb or weep for eternity or stand tall in thanksgiving for having known such fine people. It will, most likely, be a completely messed-up and unattractive combination of all three, but I know I will get through it.

I carefully made my way down the white stone steps of San Miniato and turned right down the winding street to the wide stairs that would take me back to the Arno River and across the Ponte alle Grazie. Falling into line behind three twenty-something girls, arms linked and laughing the deep, free laughter of youth, I buttoned my jacket, tightened my scarf, and smiled at the stars that twinkled above, thankful for my great life while reminding myself, for the umpteenth time, not to weaken.

TEXT: 5

Text from Katie: Part 1

Katie: Thanks for a great dinner tonight! So fun. Laura and I are still laughing about you trying to order in Italian.

   Me: So embarrassing!

   Katie: Safe journey tomorrow. Watch out for gypsies.

   Me: Will do. Sleep tight. Love you.

   Katie: Love you too.

CHAPTER 15

The Train - Part 2

I relaxed on a sky-blue fabric seat as the train rolled its way eastward toward Liguria, a northern, seaside region of Italy that hugs the Mediterranean Sea. I was going to spend two nights in Genoa-Nervi to visit the friends I had made when I lived there. The train was packed, every seat taken by people on their way. Some were dressed in workday suits, and others, like me, in garb that announced we were adventurers.

The hillsides wore the drab colors of winter, and the deciduous trees scraped at the sky with bare branches like outstretched, pleading arms. I placed the palm of my hand flat against the cold glass window to match them. The seductive motion of the train calmed me with the sense of going forward, swept by a propulsion that was not my own.

The longer you travel, the more you turn into yourself. There is a certain freedom of

expression that travel unleashes, whether you are comfortable with it or not. Stepping out of the restraints of our crowded and exhausted lives gives us wiggle room, the emotional space to examine the life that we are—or are not—leading.

The train seats were arranged in groups of four, two seats facing two with a small table in the middle. Across from me sat a young couple wearing the shiny rings of the newly married, the woman's head resting on her spouse's shoulder. To my left sat a woman who looked to be about seventy or so.

As is often the case, the four of us started a conversation sharing the reason for our travels, where we were from, and where we were headed. Indeed, the couple was on their honeymoon. The woman next me —also married yet traveling alone—and I were getting a kick out of them. Enveloped in a rosy cloud of adoration and mutual worship, they addressed each other with pats on the arm and tender "Oh, you," silly smirks. James was a lawyer, and Kerry was a research scientist at a pharmaceutical company. They shared the story of how they met, their recent wedding in California, and the upcoming honeymoon plans. They would stay a week in Portofino and a week in Rome.

Then they asked me for some marriage tips after I had shared that I had been married over twenty years. The women next to me and I shared a knowing smile. I said, "Well, I'll tell you the one thing that my mother told me. Every morning, you make the choice to be married. It is an ongoing recommitment. Love is a choice."

"That will be easy for us," Kerry giggled, squeezing James's arm.

Sure, I had plenty more to share with newlyweds, but what good would that do? All advice falls on deaf ears at that stage. The learning is in the doing. They'll have their ups and downs like everybody else. Let them bask in this extraordinary period of couplehood. Let them drink it in. All of it. Every breath of their rosy cloud, every tender caress and giggle. I can still remember my honeymoon. Innocence, Mount Gay rum, and the aquamarine waters of the Caribbean proved to be an intoxicating combination. Somehow, I believed that feeling, and the way our bodies fit together perfectly under the golden moon on a sandy beach, would last forever.

I think that everyone should bestow only good wishes and holy gestures in the presence of newlyweds. To do otherwise is cruel. A couple should trust that their love is real in that moment and powerful beyond words. That it will last forever. Because it just might. And I hope it does.

I remember the night my husband and I became engaged at a restaurant in Atlanta. Too excited to finish our meals, we jumped into his car and headed to his apartment in search of a phone (pre-cell phone era!) to share the news with our parents. On the way, we stopped to get gas at a Circle K, and I went inside to pay the cashier. I can still see her sitting on a metal stool behind the counter. She had wiry hair the color of rust, and she picked at blue nail polish that matched a tattoo that snaked around her arm. She was at least twenty years older than me, and wore a dulled, silver wedding band. I was overflowing with excitement, so I blurted my news to her as she opened the cash register. "I just got engaged!"

She looked me in the eye, took a deep breath, and counted out my change, her head shaking left and right. "Ninety-seven, ninety-eight, ninety-nine, a dollar," she said as she placed each coin carefully in the palm of my hand.

Perhaps she hadn't heard me correctly. "I just had to share the news with someone," I said. "Look!" And I held out my left hand.

She looked at my ring and said nothing. Not a word. She sat back down on the stool, grabbed a pack of Camels, and put a cigarette between her lips.

I never forgot it. Her image haunted me like a curse. I never forgave her either. Clearly her experience wasn't such a good one, but she should have at least pretended to share in my joy; should have wished me luck and let me leave that Circle K with a spring in my step rather than a backward glance through the window at a lonely creature lighting a cigarette while gazing at a black-and-white TV.

I make it a point to share the great things about marriage: the blessings, the moments when life feels real and holy and right. When your eyes meet, and something passes between you

—a knowing, a private understanding, an old joke that still makes both of you laugh. The times you roll up your sleeves and get the job done, whether it's painting a bathroom or hammering out an emotional compromise. The way you only have to say half a sentence to tell an entire story, because you just get each other. The way your couplehood has created a history that has forever marked the world in a unique way.

Why should I be the one to tell someone that there might come a day when she realizes that she misses her last name, that she is tired of checking her decisions with him? A day when she might wonder what the heck she was thinking and get teary at the fact that they don't even like to do the same things anymore. Who am I to tell her that there may come a bleak dawn when she may wake beside him and mutter something to the effect of, "Crap, he's still breathing." No, those are not the kind of things people should share with newlyweds.

I sat back and watched the young couple from the corner of my eye, his protective arm around her. What I would want to share was the one thing I wish someone had told me. That we go through stages in life so distinct that we become different people along the way.

The person we see at twenty falls away like a peeling cocoon when the thirty-year-old emerges, and then again at forty, and now I can feel it again at fifty. As we change, so do our spouses. All of this change, and the inherent friction caused by it, is cleverly disguised in the vow as "for better or for worse." If it was rephrased as "for better and during the times when we are growing and changing and find each other irritating," we'd have more to hang on to; a better understanding of the fluid and fragile nature of relationships. We'd see change for what it is: a process not an end. We might make more prudent choices to handle the dark periods when we feel out of sync and lonely.

It took me awhile to understand that relationships outgrow their paradigms. Certain world views work for an era but not forever. If a couple can push past imagined boundaries and create a new paradigm, they can breathe newness into a shared life. This understanding gave my husband and me the mind-set and framework to rebuild a marriage that had "ended" years earlier. We were able to find our way back to each other and secure a happier future for our family. Every time we sit around a table and say grace before meals, I feel a thankfulness so deep that I couldn't assign words to it if I tried.

Though there were times when I thought divorce was the best route for us, I found strength through Ecclesiastes 4:9 "Two are better than one, because they have a good return for their labor: If either one of them falls down one can help the other up. But pity anyone who falls and has no one to help them up. Also, if two lie down together, they will keep warm. But how can one keep warm alone?"

The woman next to me added her perspective, "Leave room in the marriage for each of you to be yourself as well as half of the couple. I spend money on travel, my husband spends it on golf. That's our deal and it works for us."

Ah, the things I have learned on train rides. I leaned back and rested my head as we burst out of a rather long, dark tunnel and into the sunlight. The rocky and sweeping coast of Liguria lay before us like a sparkling gift. The four of us stared, finding an inner place on which to settle as we separately marveled at the coastal beauty. Seconds turned into minutes, and we drifted into silence.

When we arrived at my stop, I stood and bid the others farewell, wishing them safe travels for their journeys in Italy and beyond. I knew that this brief intersection of our lives would stay with me somehow. The purity of a heartfelt conversation between strangers is a gift that reminds me that we are all on this human journey together.

CHAPTER 16

Camogli

My first stop in Liguria was the town of Camogli, an exquisite fishing village just east of Genoa. Elated to be back in one of my favorite spots on the planet, I ambled along its crescent-shaped shoreline. The water surged and receded in gentle fans of white foam against the beach, a bumpy carpet of flat slate stones. To my left, pelicans swooped past the craggy Aleppo pines that clung precariously to the hillsides. To the right, down the beach, stood the Basilica di Santa Maria Assunta, a two hundred-year-old church the color of sweet-cream butter.

The village is a multicolored row of buildings in mint, mango, squash, and blood orange lining the beach, tall and narrow, with open-shuttered windows like eyes that watch the sea. The tromp l'oeil facades of the buildings were so realistic that I had to decide which of the shuttered windows were real and which painted.

I dropped my backpack and sat beside it, burrowing my rear end into the stones. Two white gulls swooped overhead, and a cool breeze ruffled my hair. The late morning sun glittered on the surface of the sea, and the aural eloquence of the water, the measured rush of the waves over the stones, was hypnotic—nature's sedative.

Out of habit, I scanned the rocks nearby, picked up a stone in the shape of a heart, and let it rest in the palm of my hand. Finding them had become a family ritual over the years. Matthew and Katie had combed this beach many times in friendly competition as to who would find the most perfect one.

I wondered who might have held the stone before, who might have sat on this beach and pondered the complexities of her life. I imagined a dramatic story of an olive-skinned Ligurian beauty, the flame of youth still dimly lit in her eyes, raising a fist to the sky and cursing the moment she fell in love with a man who was owned by the sea. Who left her time and again to set sail with his first love, left her to wonder if she was wasting her days waiting. Waiting for a glimpse of his boat on the horizon, the sound of his whistle in the stairwell, the feel of his muscled arms around her waist. I imagined her tears hidden by the cloak of night when she realized that she loved a man who could read the weather, read a stormy sea and the starry sky, but could not read her heart. And finally, their long embrace when he arrived home, both relieved to be back in each other's arms.

Then, smiling to myself, I imagined myself in a long skirt with children playing at my feet, my hair pulled back by a red kerchief, scanning the horizon for the boat that carried my fisherman husband. I might romanticize such a time, but just because it was the olden days of yore doesn't mean things were always blissful. If I had lived back then I'd probably be yearning for equality, wondering why I couldn't be out there hauling nets with them. My husband would probably have rough hands and sun blisters as big as a quarter on the side of his lips. Not to mention that I'd be constantly cleaning the smell of fish out of the sheets.

Wrapping my fingers around that heart-shaped stone, I felt a kinship to every woman who had sat here before me and would come to sit here in the future. Women are deeply connected over a multitude of generations by our femininity. We know things about the business of being a woman, whether she walks the earth dressed in animal skins, corsets, hoop skirts, or hot pants. We share an understanding that transcends time and culture and words.

One of the blessings of having daughters and nieces and daughters-in-law is passing on that kinship. Watching a daughter become a woman discovering her adult strength and femininity creates another bond between us, rather than weaken the one we have now. It wraps a lasso around generations as Katie claims her link in the mighty chain that connects grandmother to mother to daughter.

Something moving at the water's edge caught my eye. At first, I thought it was a fish or a sea creature of some sort, but it was only a finger-sized piece of driftwood pointing at me, waggling in a scolding sort of way. It dredged up a memory that reminded me, again, that women must encourage each other to squeeze the life out of each moment with which we are blessed, not let the moments squeeze the life out us.

I've kept a sliver of driftwood in my bathroom drawer for thirty years. It sits amid a tumult of cosmetics that I can never keep organized. Once in a while, I'll pick it up and stare at it, turning it over slowly like I haven't examined it a thousand times already. It's shaped like a pistol, and it shoots a bullet of regret into my heart every time.

I found the driftwood one lazy summer afternoon at the Jersey Shore. I was a college student, sitting with a Cosmopolitan magazine in my lap, casually brushing up on the latest sex tips, while absentmindedly raking the sand around the edges of the frayed beach blanket. My fingers grazed a piece of soft wood a few inches deep, and I scooped it out and held it in the palm of my hand. Then I heard my name. I looked toward the dunes and saw the silvery curls of my frail grandmother, dolled up in her usual blue-and-white jumper and long-sleeved white blouse, shuffling across the sand toward me. She carried an air of determination and a smile through pursed lips that told me that she was pushing herself to the point of exertion.

I scrambled to her side, took her by the elbow, and guided her to a safe landing next to me. At some unacknowledged point over the years, she had stopped joining the family at the beach, the trek to and from our summer rental too arduous and the sun too hot on her fair Irish skin. But that day, I could sense an air of adventure, and I noted a twinkle in her eye. I loved it and was happy to have her with me, enjoying the same blue sky and breathing the same salty air.

Grandma began to reminisce about the times she and my grandfather, Millard, would stroll the boardwalk at Asbury Park. She laughed about the bathing suits they used to wear, which were longer than the dresses of today. How he loved to sit on one particular bench and light his pipe, the tobacco smoke stinging her eyes behind cat-eyed sunglasses.

At one point the scream of a frantic mother calling for her child drew our attention to the crashing waves. We watched in concerned silence as the mother searched the coast and then threw her hands in the air in relief when she spotted her daughter flat on her belly where the waves met the shore, her face mask pressed to the sand and arms stretched wide. She pulled her to her feet and hugged her with a fierceness I recall to this day, her scolding and her daughter's giggling harmonizing with the crashing of the waves and the call of the gulls.

After that my grandmother and I sat in an easy silence for a long while, looking to the sea, as neither of us was in a hurry to get back to the cottage. I watched her contemplate the late afternoon sun as it floated on the horizon—a hot, red coal that refused to be doused. Then she started a conversation for which I was ill prepared.

"I think this is the last time I will ever see the ocean," she stated in a plain, quiet voice.

"Oh, Grandma, that's not true." It shocked me, as she was never one for morbid conversation. I couldn't meet her gaze, but I watched her veined, crooked fingers straighten the edge of the blanket and sift through the sand beside it.

"The last time I will sit in the sand," she continued as if I weren't there.

My youthful self had no intention of accepting such a notion, but my soul, my old soul, had a bad feeling about it. So, I did what kids do. I pretended that it was nonsense. I pretended that life went on forever. I shut down the conversation, helped her stand, folded the blanket, and took her home as she smiled bravely, casting a final glance over her shoulder at the edge of the dune.

She was right. That was the last time she saw the ocean. A day that would stick with me forever.

The twenty-year-old me was afraid to seize the moment. Afraid that somehow, to stare truth so plainly in the face would invite an early death. The older me now knows that if we can take the moment at hand captive, it will captivate us.

Had I understood that back then, had I not let fear control that moment, I would have acted boldly. I would have said to her, "Well, if this is the last time, let's make it your best." I would have demanded that she take off her sensible shoes and walk with me to the water, support hose and all. We would have waded and let the unruly waves crash around us, cold and vital and swirling with life. We would have searched for jellyfish and not-so-perfect shells, and when we were tired, we would lay on our bellies with our faces pressed to the sand, arms and legs stretched wide, until my mother—her daughter—came to find us. Three generations of giggles would have harmonized with the soft moan of the evening wind and the crackle of the sunset bonfires being lit.

The sudden toll of the bells in the yellow church tower marked the noon hour and broke my reverie. I tucked the heart rock into my backpack, knowing I would add it to my cosmetics drawer upon my return home.

I stood, rolled the hems of my jeans to my shins, stepped gingerly over the stones, and waded out until the water, cold and vital, swirled around my ankles. Two gulls soared overhead, and the sky was impossibly blue. The rush of the waves, the soft caress of salty wind, warm winter sunshine.

Though I may never know when it will be my last time to touch the ocean, I hope it will be right here with my husband, my children, and my grandchildren beside me. I want it to be like this.

Texts from Katie: Part 2

Katie: I need to go home.

    Me: Take a deep breath.

    Katie: I'm serious. I can't do this.

    Me: Take another deep breath. Where are you?

    Katie: In class.

    Me: Which one?

    Katie: History of the Italian Mafia.

    Me: Urrgh. That class would freak me out too. I think Florence is safe.

    Katie: Where are you?

    Me: At Hotel Astor. On my way to see Annalisa.

    Katie: I wish I were there with you.

    Me: Me too.

    Katie: Okay. Just a little ripple.

Me: They'll come and go. Normal! I'll text you in a few hours. Back in two days. xoxo

CHAPTER 17

Nervi

I walked up the hill in the seaside town of Nervi toward Pizzeria Egizio. Below the glow of the sign that had hung above the corner entrance for close to forty years stood Annalisa, in a bold, unapologetic, purple cowl-necked sweater, checking her watch. She and her family live in the apartment that sat below ours when we lived here, on Via Fratelli Coda, just a block ahead. Their friendship was a blessing that saved us many a night.

"Annalisa," I called as I hurried toward her.

"You are late," she scolded, her chestnut eyes gleeful.

"Your watch is fast," I countered as she gave me a bear hug. Laughing, Annalisa pulled open the door to the pizzeria and led me in like visiting royalty. The other diners stared, their knives and forks hovering in midair over their pizzas, at the boisterous American woman who laughed and hugged Simone, Madelena, Christina, and the crew. Egizio, it turned out, was home with his new grandbaby. I was more than sorry to miss him.

The restaurant looked the same, with its freshly pressed white cotton curtains and long wooden tables. The knickknacks were on the same shelves, the framed photos still hanging on the walls. We chose the same table by the front window where Tim and I had sat with Katie and Matthew on our first mind-numbing night in Nervi.

We ordered from a menu with an exhaustive list of pizza topping combinations. Though I skimmed through it, I already knew I would order the "Daniela," topped with fresh mozzarella, tomato, Parma ham, and arugula. While we waited, we munched on baked vegetables loaded with stuffing and a spinach torta, hors d'oeuvres handmade that morning by Simone's grandmother, Giuseppina.

After Annalisa brought me up to date on her children— Elisabetta, Carlo, Esther, and Andrei—I told her about mine. Regardless of culture, our children's lives were quite similar: school, sports, clubs, and dating.

"What about Adriano?" I asked, my mouth full of torta.

Annalisa rolled her eyes as she took a spoon and waved it in front of our noses in disgust. "It is the same soup."

"What?"

"Marriage. It is the same soup. Every day." She snickered as she pulled an Italian/English dictionary the size of a shoebox from her purse, plonked it on the table, and leafed through it. "He is"—she spotted a word, then shook her head, deciding against it, and closed the book—"the same. Always." She hunched and leaned on her elbows as if to tell me a secret, but instead her voice became louder. "A man is not like a woman. He only needs sex. A woman needs love. So you may as well just have sex with him and spend his money."

As heads began to turn toward our table, she became even louder. "When we have sex, I travel to many places in my mind. Russell Crowe, in *Gladiator*, is a poster on my wall. He is my favorite travel companion."

I snorted in the midst of a gulp of wine, remembering the night I first saw that poster in her house. We had closed our eyes and sighed in unison. Annalisa had never been one to mince words, and my laughter only spurred her on to divulge a few more of her proverbs. "If he is a conquistador in bed, then you must keep him by cooking well. Notice, I am here eating pizza with you."

"Where is he, by the way? I thought he was coming with you," I said. "I was hoping to see him!"

"Adriano is home. Tired. Always tired!" She popped a generous chunk of stuffed zucchini into her mouth and chewed with gusto. "I told him this was a girls' night," she admitted. "Tim? How is Tim?" she added, a sparkle coming to her eye. She has always adored him.

"Tim is great. He sends his love," I said. "You have no idea how much he would love to be here." However, I was realizing, it was nice to be here by myself this week. I was happy with this new balance. I was finding a way to stand in the middle of the teeter-totter, one foot on both sides of my life, the individual and the partner. I was coming to peace with the separateness in the togetherness.

"I love Tim, but he is still a man," Annalisa proclaimed as she filled our wineglasses again and motioned for another carafe of the house white. Annalisa's chunky silver necklace caught the light, and she radiated energy. "This book of yours, I am in it?" she asked as Simone placed the pizzas before us.

"How could I write a book without you in it?" I asked as I cut into my crust.

"How do you say who I am?" Holding her knife and fork in each hand she powered away at the pizza.

"Well, I said a few things. Let's see . . . that you were the first neighbor to welcome us, you were generous and kind and an amazing cook and had us to dinner often. You were one of our safety nets, and you have a great laugh and—"

She cut me off with a wave of her knife. "No, no, no . . . how I look."

"Oh! Dark hair and eyes, quick smile, middle-aged woman—"

"What?" Annalisa peered at me, eyes blazing, her tone of voice so incredulous that Annie stopped mid-chew. "A middle-aged woman? What is this . . . middle-aged woman?"

"Annalisa, we're the same age. I mean, come on. We're not young."

She continued to cut her pizza with the skill of a surgeon, "But these words. They have a meaning here that is not good."

"It's not exactly wonderful in the States either, but unfortunately, if the orthopedic shoe fits . . ."

"You must change it. I will give you words."

"I can't. It's already been published."

Silence. Vigorous chewing noises. Fork and knife scraping the plate.

"Next time around you will be a goddess married to Russell Crowe."

Annalisa nodded approvingly as she quickly thumbed through her dictionary again. "Here is the word," she said proudly, displaying the page as if I could read the tiny print from across the table. "It is close to same in English, so no translation problem. Coguaro."

"Cougar? I thought the whole cougar thing was American."

"*La gallina vecchia fa buon brodo, eh?*" *The old hen makes a good broth?*

Then as the two of us coguaros ate our pizzas and

toasted the evening away, Annalisa confessed to me that while we were living in Italy, the whole neighborhood was suspicious of us. They could not understand why a family would just extricate themselves from Los Angeles and plop themselves down in the middle of Nervi. Clearly, they agreed, when they whispered to each other at the market, that intrigue had to be involved. It was general knowledge, they remarked as they passed each other on the street, that we were with the FBI, the CIA, the Witness Protection Program, or at the very least, on the lam from justice.

"I kept asking Tim, 'Why are you here?' but he would only smile over and over," Annalisa explained. "Even after I had you to our home and opened many bottles of wine, the answer was the same. 'We are here to experience life in Italy.'" She threw her hands in the air as she recalled her frustration.

So, Annalisa had worked the case month after month. She asked a friend from the *carabinieri* who was training at Quantico to search for our names on the most wanted list. When her daughter Elisabetta came to visit us in LA last summer, she told her to look through our filing cabinets when we left the house. Still nothing.

"You can stop looking now," I said between jags of laughter. "We're just boring Americans."

"Now, I am addicted to *CSI*," she said. "Adriano tells me I love the macabre. I can't help it. It crossed my mind that Tim was a . . . what do you call that . . . a serial killer."

"Stop it." I laughed as Simone brought us glasses of limoncello and two triangles of hazelnut tart.

"I have a friend," Annalisa downed the limoncello without skipping a beat, "who has an island near Saint Martin where there is a school to study cadavers. CSI techniques. I want to go there. Do you know that they keep the wine in the same refrigerators as the bodies?"

Unexpected tears sprang to my eyes as a sense of gratitude and deep joy filled me. To sit with this special woman and feel our friendship deepen despite time and distance was a gift.

"You are crying!" exclaimed Annalisa.

"Happy tears, that's all," I said, dabbing my eyes. "Hello, hormones. I don't want this night to end, I guess." Then Annalisa joined in with a few sympathy sniffles, and before we knew it, both of us were teary.

We finished our meal, kissed everyone in the pizzeria we knew (and a few we didn't!) at least three times, and I walked Annalisa the one block to her home —the same apartment building, with the gray metal balconies flat across the front, where my life changed. Where I let my emotional baggage fall from the rooftop terrace and never looked back. Where I learned that relationships can heal, and families can reclaim intimacy and successfully stride into an uncertain future together.

We stopped at the front walk, the light from the

entryway a welcoming glow. I imagined myself fishing for a key to Apartment 17 out of my pocket and following her inside. Despite my best effort at nonchalance, tears welled and dampened my cheeks.

"When will you return?" Annalisa asked.

"I don't know," I said, "but I will do my best to make it to the Ten Most Wanted list before I do."

Then she gave me another bear hug and handed me a tissue.

As I walked slowly to the old stone stairs that would take me down the hillside to the center of town, I heard Annalisa call out, "Dio veglia accanto ad ogni pianto." *God keeps watch over those who are crying.*

I turned for one last wave, and Annalisa pointed to her apartment above our heads and shouted at the top of her lungs, "Now I go to Russell Crowe!"

CHAPTER 18

Walking

Leaving Annalisa at her door, I began the descent down the first of the many staircases that crisscrossed the hillside neighborhoods of Liguria. The air was heavy, and the cloud-laden sky close and full. I passed villas and apartments with windows shuttered against the night, buttery slatted light streaming through them like glowing combs.

I had traveled these steps a thousand times. At this time of year, the foliage was spare, but during the spring and summer the vines along the walls trailed and bowed with orange trumpet flowers and purple bougainvillea. I always referred to these stairs as "my secret passageway to somewhere good." Because we didn't own a car for most of our time here, it was our route to town, our introduction to our new way of living slowly, deliberately, intentionally. That lifestyle on foot had been surprisingly grounding, no pun intended.

There was something holy about moving my body through space, about literally touching the elements every day. Warm sun, cold rain, air from the sea that could caress my cheek one minute and then slap it the next. I hadn't realized how much I needed to walk to town rather than drive, to feel the radiant heat of the worn bricks through the soles of my shoes during summer, to graze my palms along the cool, damp stone walls during fall.

I used to cherish the easy descent into Nervi in morning and then the return, grocery laden hike back up the hundreds of stairs that made my thighs burn and my gasping lungs fill with salt-laced air. I especially loved the moment when I would reach that top step, heart pounding and sweat oozing from my brow, when I would turn to catch a glimpse of cool blue water through the branches.

I can't say that every trip up and down this passageway was joyous. There were days when the four of us would tromp with moods that matched an iron sky, and evenings when fatigue made one of us bark about the injustice of life without a car. And those stormy afternoons when all I could get from my kids was an angry, incredulous what-ever-happened-to-carpool look as we turned our faces upward and counted the steps aloud while we headed home in a downpour without umbrellas.

We attain a sense of intimacy with our surroundings and gain wisdom by walking. Walkers see things, tiny details of lives that otherwise go unnoticed, the rhythms of families and couples and those who live alone. In noticing, you begin to care when you see new baby clothes pinned to the line, or a fastidiously tidy stoop that suddenly goes unswept. You notice when a person might need you to stop and lend a hand or give a cheery hello to brighten a quiet and long afternoon. You begin to matter.

I navigated the hairpin curve of a road that would take me to a second set of stairs, hidden along a tangled hedge farther ahead. Passing an iron gate, locked for the night, I paused. Behind it was a tiny chapel with a statue of the Blessed Virgin Mary standing sentinel by the door. The adjacent garden slept, waiting for the warm breath of spring. Approaching the gate, I grabbed hold of the cast-iron bars like I was a prisoner inside a cell. I love this little chapel. I still dream about it. Standing quietly, the night wrapped itself around me. A gauzy mist wafted in smoky whirls around dim lights illuminating the property in a reverent, ethereal glow.

Continuing on, I passed a few more villas and started down the second staircase. Soon I was on the coast road heading back toward my hotel. The sea roared and crashed in the dark, inky and troubled. The mist thickened into a fog that played hide-and-seek in the alleys.

Funny, I had not felt a sense of fear since I landed in Italy. I don't know what to attribute that to, but I have always felt safe in this town. Have always opted for the long walk home after an evening out with family or friends. Some nights the moon was a polished gold coin that hovered above the waves. Tonight, however, the heavens were a flat black, and pregnant with rain. Lightning cracked the sky at the horizon.

Though I was finding spiritual and emotional nourishment and greatly enjoying my time alone, I felt Tim's presence walking with me. I missed him. Marriage is a complicated mixture of alone and together. Like the opposite poles of two magnets—sometimes you attract each other and other times you repel. Sometimes we need to walk alone, and sometimes we need to walk together. I am making peace with the jagged edges that define relationships. We are perfectly imperfect together. And that is okay. We have stopped putting so much pressure on each other.

I passed a stretch of shops closed for the night. Each one held the histories of a family. Generations that rose each day to play their part in a community. The butcher, the pasta maker, the hardware store owner, the baker, the optician, the barista. I wondered if I sat in one of these shops alone at midnight if it would whisper to me of the loves and losses of the ancestors who had wiped its counters and stocked its shelves.

I came to another stretch of road near a popular gelato shop, where a few benches faced the sea. Then to the alley that opened into the old port of Nervi. It was a picturesque little port, like so many that lined the coast of Liguria. A mixture of apricot-colored apartments, restaurants, cafes, and small boats turned upside down for the winter, their white bellies exposed.

I ambled a few yards to the water's edge where the waves lapped gently and sighed at the lonely beauty. The port was a monochrome, deep with fog. The glow of an occasional streetlamp illuminated the cascading mist. I almost expected Humphrey Bogart to round the corner in a trench coat and light a cigar. Except for waves crashing beyond the break, it was quiet—a middle-of-the-night quiet that held dreams and night-mares in secret places. The temperature had dropped considerably, and I could see my breath. Plucking a stone from the shoreline, I said a prayer for our marriage and threw it into the sea, waiting to hear the satisfying kerplunk when it hit the surface.

I stood for a long time and listened to the waves, to the wind, and to the centuries of human longing. The truth of the matter, I was coming to understand, was that a marriage includes lonely moments like this one. We will always feel a deep yearning for something more intimate whether we are married or not. Sometimes the yearning is subtle, like a thirst that nags even when you have just finished a glass of water. Sometimes it rears itself so loudly you can't help but go in search of someone who can quench it. But it never goes away, even when you think you've found the one, or the second one, or the third. Another human being will never be able to provide enough love to quench that eternal desire because it is the hole in us that God created for himself. Our hunger for it reminds us to seek him. Only he can bring us that completion, that sense of peace. Marriage was about seeking him together.

I have missed the surge and crash of these waters and the briny scent of the air, but what I have missed most—what I have been seeking without knowing it—was the state of grace that surrounded our couple-hood here, when we admitted our fragility to each other and surrendered to God's lead. I need to work on getting back to that. There is really no other way I want to live.

Texts from Home: Part 5

Tim: Hi, Honey. Just got home from work. Sick of the grind. Exhausted. Thinking about running to Home Depot for a few more things.

Me: Just relax! Have a glass of vino. Chores can wait.

Tim: I see you're settling in.

Me: Saw Annalisa and the gang at Egizio's tonight. Everyone asked for you.

Tim: You're so lucky.

Me: Feeling peaceful.

Tim: I should have come.

Me: I miss you. Serious this time.

Tim: I miss you. Serious this time, too :)

CHAPTER 19

Seeking Adventure

The next morning, the manager of the Hotel Astor eyed me with suspicion as I walked through the lobby buttoning my coat. I nodded and smiled, knowing he must be wondering where I could be headed at 4:45 a.m. on a misty February morning. For some reason sleep was impossible, so I decided to watch the sun rise on the Mediterranean, for old time's sake.

Turning right onto Viale delle Palme, I headed toward the water, flipping my collar against the cold and giving my scarf an extra wrap around my head. Like an aimless ghost, a patch of cloud slid along the top of the empty train station two blocks ahead, illuminated by street lamps and a glimmer of light from inside the building. It was too early even for the trains.

Nervi is famous for the winding and breathtaking Passeggiata Anita Garibaldi, a wide brick walkway that hugs the rocky coastline. It had been an intimate part of my life when I lived here—a safe place to wander, to wonder, and to while away many an afternoon. I knew that the sloping path to the right of the train station was an entrance to it.

My eyes slowly adjusted to the silhouettes of the buildings and trees against the indigo sky, and my feet navigated the uneven sidewalk. I ventured cautiously through the alley that ran beneath the train tracks, thankfully, finding it empty except for the echoes of the restless surf beyond. It was like walking through a conch shell that whispers of its previous life when you hold it to your ear.

The wind bit my nose and cheeks as I stepped onto the passeggiata and shuffled across the red brick to claim a weathered blue bench beneath the dim glow of a gas lamp. I folded my arms against the ocean spray, my face frozen into a grimace.

With a deep sigh, I looked to the distant horizon and drank in 180 degrees of the quiet, silvery beauty of the gray dawn. Whitecaps, like fingernails, scratched the surface of the water, dark as slate under a clouded sky that was slowly transforming into a mosaic of old nickels and new dimes with the first light.

There was a time when I loathed gray days. Saw them as the guest who ruined the party. Gray was dented steel and slush, pollution spewing from smokestacks, the howl of the preying coyote. Gray was trouble; it meant you were lost. As a young woman, I refused to live in shades of gray. I wanted street signs and carefully marked routes through life. I wanted clarity, reds and blues and fiery oranges all the time. Colors that knew what they were.

A gull appeared and dipped toward the water where a seal raised its head to greet it. In the distance a lightening in the cloud cover hinted of the sun hiking up the back side of the Portofino promontory. At the suggestion of daybreak, the hues of the morning changed, and the dance of metals invited other colors to the waltz. The tones deepened with greens and purples, and the sky grabbed a soft bruised yellow and tucked it among its folds.

Such were the limits of the youthful me. Time reveals new definitions about the matters of color, and I now understood that gray carries a heavenly weight. It is the color of trust, patience, courage, and wisdom. The anchor in the storm, the soldier's uniform, the surgeon's tools, and a grandmother's hair curled for Easter Sunday. It is knowledge and experience, the sole of a shoe that has walked half the earth. It is the transformative power of surrender.

I closed my eyes and took a deep breath, tasting the piquant tang of the air. I thought about one of Genoa's beloved sons, Christopher Columbus, and how he had learned to sail right here on these waters. I'm sure he had his share of dark, uncertain days, but he must have suspected that gray was also the color of adventure, the hue assigned to times when we are sustained only by faith and hope, when we're sailing on a sea of question marks searching for reasons, a purpose, an answer, a new home. He must have known it was the color of becoming—a person who sets out to find new routes around the world can't be afraid of the fog. Being lost is the beginning of the journey to being found.

Now, I am sensing a spiritual shift from needing absolutes to craving mystery. I must look forward to gray periods of disequilibrium as opportunities for growth and adventure. The word *adventure*, finding its root in the Latin word *adventura*, means "about to happen." This week has reminded me to be open to that which is about to happen. To stop trying to control the outcome and lay to rest the notion that I must know where my life is going all the time. I must once again put "what is about to happen" back into the hands of God.

As theologian Frederick Buechner so beautifully stated in *Wishful Thinking: A Theological ABC*, "The place God calls you to is the place where your deep gladness and the world's deep hunger meet." I am regaining my sense of trust in the going forward. My path will be revealed in its time. I am ready, again, to relax and enjoy the adventure of my future.

Hugging my knees against my chest, I savored the rush of wind through the trees, the thrust of the sea against jagged black rock, and the distant moan of a steamship in Genoa's harbor down the coast. The round disc of the sun pressed into the clouds like a flashlight behind a white sheet. My buddy the seal awakened a friend, and now there were two heads bobbing in the waves. An early riser jogged by with a rhythmic slap of his running shoes against the brick walkway, and we nodded to each other, knowing we were sharing this moment of beauty.

The light in the sky increased, and an unexpected strip of blue appeared through a parting of clouds. The sound of voices and the aroma of coffee found their way on the breeze, and the hum of a distant train reminded me that I was catching the 8:10 back to Florence. I rose from the bench as golden rays pierced the cloud cover at last, blew a kiss to my beautiful sea, and walked happily up the brick path toward the unknown.

Texts from Katie: Part 3

Katie: Are you back in Florence yet?
  Me: Just checked back into hotel.
  Katie: Meet us at the market? 4 leoni tonight? A new friend said to try the pear gorgonzola ravioli.
  Me: Perfetto! Delicious!
  Katie: You mean delizioso?
  Me: Yes, that's what I meant. :)
  Katie: E vino bianco?
  Me: Si, si. You are feeling better?
  Katie: Si, si, si :)

CHAPTER 20

Gelato

After a heartwarming dinner of minestrone, pear gorgonzola ravioli and a glass of rich Chianti with Katie and Laura, I ambled back toward the Hotel De Lanzi along Via dei Calzaioli. The gray and white marble of the Duomo rose stark and ghostly against a stormy sky like an artist's charcoal rendering come to life. The evening was quiet and still with ribbons of mist gathering at its edges. It had been a grace-filled day, and I didn't want it to end.

The girls and I had sauntered through Florence's famous outdoor markets. We grabbed a few new scarves to add to our wardrobes; I picked up leather belts and wallets for Tim and Matthew; and we enjoyed a day of wandering through cobblestoned alleyways and side streets, stopping for photos along the way. They were happily settling in.

The glow from a gelato shop up ahead illuminated the corner at Via del Campanile, a block from my hotel. The store was uncharacteristically empty as it usually attracted a constant stream of customers from morning to night. Italian customers, not tourists, so I knew it had to be the real deal. The word GROM, in plain block letters, was etched above the door. Gelato, I decided, would be a fitting way to top off the night.

I walked toward the glow watching the lone scooper inside wiping counters and preparing to close. It reminded me of the job I had had as a teen at Grunings, a German ice cream and candy store on Bloomfield Avenue in Montclair, NJ. Two of my brothers and I worked there together after school and on weekends. Getting paid to dish ice cream, chat up the customers, and eat hot fudge sundaes on our short breaks hardly felt like work. The grumpy German owner would scold us for laughing too much, harping that we didn't take our careers seriously; and how many times did he have to show us how small the scoops were supposed to be to turn a profit?

Pulling the door open, I entered and the employee, in his pistachio and raspberry stained white apron, nodded and smiled. Middle-aged, he had blond wavy hair and warm eyes the color of toast.

"Ciao. Buona sera." I pulled out my best accent.

"Ciao, Signorina."

"Non, Signora," I corrected him as he smiled an "Aren't I a charmer" smile.

He opened his arms wide to show the array of gelato canisters. "Abbiamo molti gusti." *We have many flavors.*

"Stracciatella?" *Chocolate chip?*

"Si. Quanto?"

"Medio," I said as I pointed to the medium sized cup. He grabbed an ice cream scoop, opened the container, and scooped with vigor. Just before he closed the lid he hesitated with a dramatic air, then winked at me as he put an illegal third scoop into the cup.

"Un uomo dei miei sogni!" *A man of my dreams!* I exclaimed, and we shared a laugh. As he placed the small white cup in my outstretched hand, I was suddenly standing at Applegate Farms, another ice cream destination that was a special family treat during my childhood. After dinner, on balmy summer evenings as the lightning bugs traced figure eights in the dark, we would pile into the wood paneled station wagon and drive a few miles down Grove Street to the historic farm with the big red barn. That was the best. Standing in line, reading the flavors, discussing which one we'd choose when it was our turn with the seriousness of diplomats at the UN. The eight of us, licking away in silence, delirious with happiness for a moment until…someone's scoop would plop to the pavement and our collective gasp would silence the crowd.

I paid a few euro and plucked a tiny plastic spoon

from the counter. "Grazie, Signore," I said as I raised my cup in salute.

"Prego, prego. Ciao e buona notte."

"Buona notte."

I headed outside. The air was now cold, but instead of walking to my hotel, I chose to lean against a building nearby. Resting the back of my head against the stone wall, I closed my eyes and breathed in the night. Wind in my ears, distant traffic, a woman's throaty laughter. As I took another bite of gelato, I heard a multitude of feet pattering. Turning to peer down the street, I glimpsed the ghosts of young boys, my brothers, running toward our kitchen freezer, shoving each other, arms outstretched.

Move over! What's left? You already had two bowls. Stop pushing. Mom! Todd just whacked me in the head. Tattle-tale!

From that moment, every spoonful of gelato awakened family memories that had been peacefully sleeping for decades. It was not the first time I had been sidelined with nostalgia. These episodes of intense reminiscence were often born of daily occurrences like this one, as simple as setting the table, going for a bike ride, or playing cards. I find them comforting, amusing, and unsettling. For some reason I am deeply missing my family. Not the people I know now as adults, but the ones I knew forty years ago when we shared a modest, four-bedroom house.

I grew up in a male world. Five brothers and a

larger-than-life father whom I felt counted as two people. My mother and I stuck together like glue, two drops of estrogen in a testosterone sea. It was an era of dairy products. All of those growing bones and muscles needed protein and calcium, and we collectively consumed a minimum of two gallons of milk per day. Coupled with an assortment of cheeses, butter, and frozen confections, we were a veritable mucous and gas factory which, in a house full of boys, was deemed a great thing. It gave us all something to talk and laugh about, ad nauseam.

Ice cream ruled the freezer and our lives. It divided us, united us, and sent us on family outings. It taught us to share, to bargain, and to thank. It made TV more fun to watch and a sore throat bearable. Magical and medicinal, it calmed our nerves, soothed our broken hearts, and saved us from childhood fears.

It also taught us to sneak and lie.

Who left this dirty bowl shoved under the couch? Not me. Who ate the last ice cream cup? Not me. Who put the empty carton back in the freezer? Not me.

Six children spanned a period of twelve years. Todd, Kevin, and I were like The Three Stooges. Our older brothers, David and Tim, being infinitely wiser and in a separate class of coolness altogether, barely acknowledged us. Joe was born when I was seven making him more of a plaything to us, someone to dress up and boss around.

We Three Stooges were serious about controlling

the influx of ice cream into the house. Our fights at the grocery freezer were legendary, standing before the freezer section hips square, balled fists, chins jutting forward in a challenge. We just had mint chip. Vanilla is boring. Rocky road, butter pecan? Can't we try coffee? That tastes like puke. Neapolitan? No one eats the strawberry.

My mother's long arm would end the argument cutting through the circle and reaching for whatever flavor was closest to her. For some reason we only got one tub at a time. I am not sure what her thinking was since one tub lasted exactly fourteen minutes. Somehow, we all knew how much each person ate. We had a thing about fairness, and it was a relief when she would come home with individually wrapped ice cream bars, sandwiches, or Popsicles, so we could do some quick math to decide how many each person was allowed to have to make it even. Odd numbers threw us into a tizzy, usually solved by putting our closed fists into a circle. One potato, two potatoes, three potatoes, four.

In those days, the Ice Cream Man was more popular than the Pope; a godlike creature who circled the globe in a magic truck with an endless supply of creamy confection. The bells could be heard blocks away, giving us just enough time to race through the house hunting for coins. Perhaps, it could be said that some were stolen from the small blue ceramic bowl on my father's dresser in these-stress filled moments, but I wouldn't swear on it in court.

As I shaved tiny slivers of the chocolate speckled gelato and let it melt on my tongue, I studied the time-worn buildings, their arched doorways and the shuttered windows above them. I loved the way the street names were etched in stone on the corners of buildings. Two policemen straddled atop sleepy horses nodded to me as they plodded by, iron horseshoes on cobblestone.

Smiling and wistful, I scraped the last of the stracciatella from the sides of the cup and sighed. "Good old chocolate chip," I said aloud to the empty street conjuring the distant echo of a heated discussion we had had at the dinner table one night over the merits of finely ground chips vs. large chocolate chunks. Any flavor could place me somewhere along the continuum of my childhood. My father loved butter pecan, my mother always ordered chocolate, Breyers vanilla fudge whisked me to my best friend Trevor's, sunny TV room and sat us side by side with tiny spoons eating from the carton.

A fine rain began to fall, and my toes called for warmth, but I couldn't bring myself to move because I knew that if I did, my ice cream memories would disappear. My recollections would fade and blend with the mist. My brothers would run away. So, I stood a long time in the soft rain.

As so aptly stated by William Herbert Carruth, "Memory breeds in me a strange loneliness." I yearn for my childhood. I didn't expect to grieve it now after all of these years. It scares me, realizing that so much of my life is already gone. So much of who my brothers are to me, is gone. Over. They are now grown men with families and complicated lives, but I still hold them close to my heart, locked in that singular era. We are now a family scattered across the country, but when we get together we recall the same stories again and again, never tiring of the power of shared history to keep us connected, to keep those six mischievous children happily playing board games and watching the Mary Tyler Moore Show for the rest of our days.

I threw my cup and spoon into a nearby trash can and slowly walked toward my hotel noting my reflection in the glass doors of the shops that I passed, one quite different from the naive young woman behind the lunch counter at Grunings who flirted with customers and dated the handsome police officer who came in every day for a milkshake. The girl who used to dream big.

What is it about life that draws us backwards? The loss of that era weighs upon me so heavily that it fills me with fear that I did not do enough for my own children. Crossing the street, my hair slick and my clothes damp, I prayed that I have blessed them with memories powerful enough to haunt them when they are fifty and floundering. What if I haven't?

I opened the door to the hotel, stepped out of my past into the light and warmth of the present. I nodded to the night clerk, his balding head bent over a book. As I headed toward the stairs that would take me to my third-floor room, he called after me, "We have umbrellas." He pointed to a stack of them in a container by the door.

I turned, our eyes meeting, "Non era un problema. E 'stata una bella pioggia." *Not a problem. It was a fine rain.*

"Ah," he said, nodding slowly, thoughtfully. "Si, perfetto. Buona notte, Signorina."

"Signora," I corrected him as we shared a smile. "Buona notte, Signor," I said as he went back to his book, and I continued up the stairs.

CHAPTER 21

Seeking Gratefulness

Sunshine surged up crooked streets, a rising tide of light and energy, as the final residue of a midnight rain evaporated from awnings, storefronts, and stone. The chatter of neighbors and shopkeepers sweeping stoops and teasing each other filled me with the anticipation of a day not yet lived. This would be my last morning in Florence before I said good-bye to Katie and headed to Rome and then home. I decided to go to the Uffizi, one of the world's most important museums for Italian art. The rhythm of my boots against damp cobblestones clicked like an antique metronome marking tiny slices of four-four time. Though it was a major thoroughfare, Via dei Calzaiuoli was not crowded, and I enjoyed a steady pace.

Though I have been to Florence a few times, I had yet to set foot inside the Uffizi. Not because I didn't want to, but because I am unable to enjoy art if a museum is so crowded that I can smell the person standing beside me. I still shudder when I remember experiencing the Sistine Chapel on the same day as thousands of other admirers. By the time I arrived inside the chapel all I could think about was getting out. If the lines were too long for the Uffizi, I'd spend the morning elsewhere.

There is something intimate about paintings and sculpture that demands space to appreciate. I would rather pass on the opportunity to walk through the Uffizi than ruin a lifetime of exquisite anticipation. When I finally stand before Botticelli's masterpiece, *The Birth of Venus*, I don't want to hear someone else's breathing, the crunch of a granola bar, or the casual dismissal of a painting that I have treasured for most of my life. I want to look into Venus's light-brown eyes and remember the enchantment I felt the first time I saw an image of her illuminating the pull-down projector screen of a college classroom.

As I rounded the bend, I gasped as I took in the most unexpected sight. The Piazzale degli Uffizi, with its narrow courtyard and stately colonnades, was nearly empty. Not a line in sight. I hurried to the entrance and tried the handle, wondering if it was closed. "This is crazy," I said aloud as the door opened. I was finally getting my date with Botticelli.

Suddenly, I couldn't move my feet. Heat flushed my skin, and my heart jumped into my throat. I was unexpectedly overcome with an odd combination of awe and dread. Now that I was here, I was almost afraid to look. What if my favorite painting was a letdown? What if coming face-to-face with Venus, goddess of beauty, dredged up all sorts of memories or feelings of inadequacy that I had invested precious time and good energy into suppressing?

I bought a ticket, studied a map handed to me by a guard with a chipped front tooth and a warm smile, and ascended a few flights of white marble stairs. The Uffizi ("the Offices") was originally built by Duke Cosimo I de' Medici to house the offices of the palace next door. It is U-shaped with two long, narrow wings joined by a hallway on the south end.

Except for a few people scattered about, I was deliciously, incredibly alone. I stood at the end of a seemingly endless, talcum-colored hallway with a polished black-and-white tile floor. The gallery rooms, twenty-four of them, were on the left. The right wall was a series of windows, tall thin rectangles of diffused white light. Along the walls, between doorways and windows, stood marble busts and statues on black pedestals, lined in a row like soldiers under frescoed ceilings. It used to irk me that these famous, powerful people would hire artists to paint their pictures or carve elaborate statues, but not anymore. They were merely human beings, using the only means they had to touch eternity. Don't we all want that in one form or another?Appreciating that I was on artists' holy ground, I walked reverently forward. This place was filled with ghosts. The good kind. The silence here was loud.

Museums for me, are not solely about the canvases that hang on the walls. Not only about the chiseled sculpture and expert knowledge of color, design, texture, or subject matter. Museums are also about the human beings that created the works. I imagined scores of restless artisans crisscrossing the tiles with rainbow-smudged palettes and paintbrushes caked with pigment, calloused hands speckled with marble dust, and ringed eyes from sleepless nights and days of arduous work. I sensed them here, wishing they could add one more detail, one more brushstroke, a little color here or a dab there, one more of something to make it perfect.

I had plenty of time before I met Katie for lunch, so I decided to take a walk through the Middle Ages first. Slowly, luxuriously, I entered Room 2 and gazed around a large high-ceilinged, white-walled room featuring altarpieces painted on wood by Giotto, Cimabue, and Duccio. Much of the art during the Middle Ages had been commissioned for religious purposes—depictions of biblical scenes to adorn great basilicas or simple chapels.

Unexpectedly, I came upon Giotto's *Ognissanti Madonna*, more than two decades after I chose it as the subject of a semester project. I stood before it, awed. I had forgotten about it, but here it was, as real as me. In college I had chosen this painting to research because I was fascinated at the thought that the beginning of an entire period in art history could be traced to a single work. Time must pass for historians to be able to look backward and compare artists. Sometimes an entire lifetime goes by before they can place a collective index finger on an image and say, "This is the one."

Generally considered the painting that heralded the Renaissance, *Ognissanti Madonna* features Mary, the Christ child on her lap, and various angels. The figures are three-dimensional, a great departure from the Byzantine style of the time, communicating a sense that mere humans had something in common with God. That the heavens were not an unreachable parade of saints but figures that looked like us. Giotto gave humans hope that they could have a relationship with the divine.

Back in college, I probably spent pages and pages exploring style, composition, and artistic tradition, but I am quite sure that I did not think about Giotto in simple human terms. An artist who decided one day to boldly break tradition, to use his unique perspective and vision in a way that would begin an era that would change the Western world. Such refreshing audacity. A holy effrontery.

I became perturbed with the stark walls of the

room. Something about it felt wrong, like seeing a Christmas decoration for sale in July. After some thought, I realized that I yearned to see this altarpiece hanging in the church it had originally occupied, to see it fulfilling its purpose as a vessel to lift praying souls to heaven, not as an end in itself, hanging by a wire on a wall. Though I understood the effectiveness of a quiet backdrop to highlight this great work, it took the art away from its home, its purpose, like taking a bucket away from the well.

I walked through the Flamboyant Gothic Room (nothing was anywhere near flamboyant in my narrow opinion), the Early Renaissance Room, and the Filippo Lippi Room (where I noticed a few royal-blue walls . . . scandalous). Between each gallery, I studied the busts in the hallway of famous Florentines, mythical figures, and politicians, their eyes smooth stone in storied faces.

Then I was there, at the entrance to the Botticelli Room, larger than the others with a raised dark-wood ceiling and a cinnamon-tiled floor. Just a few feet away, without fanfare, was *The Birth of Venus*.

Walking gently, so that my boots would not intrude on this quiet wonderfulness, I made my way over to it. I studied every inch, every brushstroke, imagining Botticelli in a candlelit studio at midnight adding pink roses falling from the sky as the perfect finishing touch. If the canvas were not protected by a plate of Plexiglas, I would have wrapped my arms around it. As a young woman, I was entranced by this depiction of the goddess of beauty. She is positively luminous, an elegant creature with long blonde tresses blowing in the wind, and nary a tangle in sight. Having just emerged whole and luscious from the sea, she is gently blown ashore on a shell by the wind gods and welcomed with a lovely cloak by one of the Hours.

This painting speaks to me of beauty, poetry, and purity. It exudes feminine power and mystery. As a college sophomore, I loved it. I wanted to *be* Venus. I didn't realize, back then, that I *was* her, as are all young women cloaked in innocence. How could I have known I was her when I lacked the confidence to stand alone in a shell buoyed by the sea? What does any young woman truly know of the power of youth?

I remember sitting in my dorm room in a plaid flannel shirt, leaning against a painted cinder-block wall while I thumbed through a course list, trying to finalize my choices for the upcoming semester. Though I was registered as a political science major, I knew it meant nothing to me. The coursework stayed in my head and never touched my heart. It was all theory—explainable and quotable.

I had a fine arts credit to fill, and I chose, for no apparent reason, an art history course. It would require two semesters of lugging an enormous red book entitled *Art Through the Ages* around campus. The book still sits on a shelf in my office.

I knew nothing about art back then. A big fat zero. I was blessed, however, with a professor who was filled with unbridled passion about a world that was new to me. The course introduced me to a new language, a wordless one: the language of heart and soul.

We started our journey in ancient Mesopotamia and ended in twentieth-century America. I had never felt more alive in a classroom. It was endlessly hard work: the papers, the lectures, the discussions, the memorizing of countless slides of artists and their creations. The visual history of the world taught me things about myself and human nature that I wonder now, if I would ever have understood otherwise. You can talk about myth, religion, power, love, passion, and heartbreak all you want, but it is altogether different to see it splayed across a canvas or painstakingly etched into stone. *The Dying Gaul* was the first piece of marble to make my heart break. It would not be the last.

It was in that art history class that I began to understand that life evolves in apprenticeships—child to the parent, student to the teacher, beginner to the mentor—and that eras do end. I plainly saw that though people sometimes seek to re-create the golden glow of days gone by, it never happens. A new era may be built upon the pedestal of previous knowledge, but new artists add a layer of evolved thought, the colors of a changed world.

In front of *The Birth of Venus*, I took a step backward for some perspective, then another and another until I felt the cold, flat bench in the center of the room press into the soft skin behind by knees. That's when I noticed it. That beautiful, ethereal visage did not look happy. Venus's face was passive, her eyes devoid of emotion, not even Mona Lisa's hint of a smile.

I glanced over my shoulder to regard Botticelli's *Primavera* on another wall. In this equally famed painting, an older Venus stands amid a virtual springtime garden party: The Three Graces dancing on one side and Flora throwing flowers on the other, Cupid flying above, Mercury reaching for an orange, and Chloris in the woods with Zephyr. Again, in the midst of this display of sensuality and fertility, there are no smiles. I sensed, in this painting, the urgency of sexuality, but no real joy.

I sat down on that cold, flat bench, and an enormous sense of relief washed over me. I let go of the sadness about the passing of years. My Venus era was a memory, and from my midlife perspective, I could see that youth was a heady and delicious time of life for me, but it was not my happiest.

I sat on the bench in quiet contemplation for a long time. When a dream comes true, even one as small as meeting a favorite painting face-to-face, I like to drag it out as long as possible. It makes me hopeful that other dreams will also come true. Then, rising to my feet, I knew my date with Botticelli was over. I quietly clasped the palms of my hands together in dismissal.

I headed down the east wing and, at the end of the

hall, turned right into another corridor. I came to a window that overlooked the Arno River below and paused to admire the shimmer of the morning sunlight on the water. I felt grateful in a way that was renewing me. Happy in a way that held promise.

CHAPTER 22

A Time to Let Go - Part 3

I stood alone in the Piazza del Duomo, waiting for Katie. It was time to say good-bye. Time for her to begin her adventure abroad without a safety net. Time for both of us to step off the bridge. I spotted her moving toward me in a sea of people, her slender six-foot frame buttoned into a pine-green jacket. With a pumpkin-colored scarf wrapped around her neck, and her gleaming blonde hair pulled into a ponytail, she looked like a model from a magazine instead of my little girl. I gave her a hug. Words were not necessary.

We entered an elegant coffee shop with brightly lit glass cases filled with lunch fare, as well as gelato and desserts for every taste. Katie ordered cappuccino and a brioche, and I ordered a panini. We took seats opposite each other at a highly lacquered wooden table.

Small dark circles under her eyes suggested a restless night. She sipped her coffee and picked at the pastry, and I noticed that she kept glancing at a clock on the wall above my head.

We couldn't look too deeply into each other's eyes, because then we would have to say real things. This good-bye had to be breezy.

"Are you all unpacked?" I asked. Katie had only two suitcases, and we'd unpacked them together; of course, she was unpacked.

"Mostly. A few things left. We don't have much storage, so I might just leave some stuff in the suitcase."

"How's the coffee? You're not eating."

"My stomach hurts," she said as she pushed the plate to the side. An old soul, born with a gift of wisdom far beyond her years, she was the type of teen who understood that the open caverns inside of her, which she used to fill with me, now needed to be filled with her own separate sense of self. Her own ideas and passions. She needed to develop her own definitions of who she was and what type of woman she wanted to become. It was time to walk alone.

"I'm afraid for you to leave," she said, challenging me not to desert her.

"You're going to be fine. You've got your two closest friends here with you. You'll learn to take care of each other."

"I want to be a person who travels fearlessly and has these . . . you know, great world adventures, someone who works in exotic places."

"You are that person. Look where you are!" I spread my arms wide as she wrapped hers around her stomach.

"Then why do I want to burst out crying?" Her eyes teared. "It isn't easy."

"It's not easy for anyone. Who said it was going to be easy?"

"But I wake up at night and feel alone."

"We all do."

"I don't know my way around. I might get lost."

"You'll figure it out."

"I know one thing in my head, another in my heart, but feel only panic and fear in my stomach. I just want them all to connect."

"Oh, honey, that's part of the journey of faith." Where was I coming up with all of these answers? Who was I kidding? I wanted to scoop her into my arms and take her home.

Time slid into early afternoon, and soon I had to leave for the train station. We wandered outside, asked a woman to snap our picture together, and pasted on big smiles. Then the moment was there.

"Well, honey," I said as I brushed back her bangs and pulled her scarf tight against the cold. "You are strong and smart . . ."

"No, Mom. We're not going to do this."

"Okay. I love you. Have fun. Be brave."

"I love you too."

Off she walked, on unsure feet, until she blended into a bustling crowd heading down an Italian street. Though I stood for a long time with my arm in the air, she never turned for one last wave.

CHAPTER 23

The Cathedrals Within

After a whirlwind six-hour tour of Rome, a small triumph in the history of tourism, my taxi pulled to the curb at the entrance to Saint Peter's Square on Via della Conciliazione. I had arrived at Roma Termini early that morning, stowed my bag in a luggage holding room, and headed down Via Cavour. A few cab rides to strategic locations and landmarks, a few lively sprints, and a few espressos later, I decided that Vatican City would be a fitting way to end the day.

I handed six euros to the driver and climbed out. Ahead of me, at the far end of the piazza, loomed the magnificent and imposing facade of Saint Peter's Basilica. Like two great arms reaching for me, semicircular symmetrical colonnades, four columns deep and forty feet tall, lined both sides. If Gian Lorenzo Bernini, the architect who designed the piazza, was hoping to awe future generations of visitors, he had certainly accomplished his goal.

The sun slipped behind the massive dome, smearing the sky with copper and salmon and sending the piazza into a swirl of warm shadows. I walked to the Egyptian obelisk that rose proudly in the center of the piazza. Composed of red granite, the obelisk is eighty-three feet high and topped with a cross.

This structure witnessed the death of Saint Peter. Over thirty-eight hundred years old, the obelisk was brought to Rome in AD 37 and stood for years in the center of the Circus of Nero, which was the emperor's private circus, where he hosted horse races as well as the martyrdom of Christians. Now it stands here watching us.

The lights around the piazza began to glow. I gazed upward and studied the obelisk—so sure of itself, relieved to have found a peaceful resting place after all the violence to which it had been privy.

I searched the Apostolic Palace and located the second window on the right, where the Pope comes each Sunday to pray the Angelus and bless the crowd. The last time I stood here, one in a crowd of thousands, I listened to Pope John Paul II. Though I didn't understand the language he spoke, I sensed his holiness. Felt the lift of grace so strongly that my soul hovered above the concerns of the flesh.

I wondered, for a sacrilegious moment, how he had felt about getting older. Was it easier to age if you were the Catholic Church's number one man? Had he had private moments of angst about under-eye bags and stooping shoulders? I would have appreciated hearing about that in one of his papal addresses.

Spotlights turned on across the top of the facade, beacons in the darkness, bringing to life the statues of the apostles that stood across the top. It was getting late, so I headed toward the entrance. As I entered the nave of the basilica, I stood, motionless, absorbing the immensity of the space. The basilica was so expansive that a fifteen-story building could fit inside, but because of its perfect dimensions, it did not overpower. Dusk was upon me, and there were no crepuscular rays streaming through the windows of the dome above to illuminate or call me forward. The cathedral was dark, candles flickered, and a quiet rush of grace pressed against me.

The interior encompasses 215,000 square feet of marble, sculpture, paintings, and mosaics. The floors, columns, and walls were an array of polished granite in reds and grays, and veined marbles in cinnamon, black, white, and green. Beneath the gilt-coffered ceiling, ornate altars lined each side wall, and straight ahead of me, Bernini's massive bronze canopy, the *Baldacchino*, towered above the papal altar, the focal point of the church. I walked forward and counted the marks on the floor that depicted where other whole cathedrals would fit inside this one: Saint Paul's in London, Saint Patrick's in New York, Notre-Dame in Paris, and the Duomo in Florence. Catholic or not, no one can deny that this church is mighty—a fearsome and thunderous statement. The burial place of popes and saints. Every church speaks to me of God, but this one proclaims to me: *I am vast, I breathe grace, I hold within me man's proudest moments and greatest works.*

I felt smaller than I had in years. It felt good, surprisingly. Safe. Like a child who had walked into her house after a long vacation, happy to be home.

Through all of my adventures this past week, I realized that it was only in the various churches I visited that I had felt completely at home and free. Able to fully relax and let my guard down. Let myself yearn in plain view—my fears and my truths commingled in awkwardly worded prayer and in pregnant silences that revealed more than my words could communicate.

I was drawn immediately to the Chapel of the Pietà. Behind bulletproof glass stood Michelangelo's famous sculpture, carved from a single block of Carrara marble. It depicts a seated Mary with the body of her son draped across her lap after he was taken down from the cross. Her face is serene, yet deeply sad. She holds him, tenderly, this full-grown man, like the child that he was to her. Her baby, her teen, her courageous and wise boy who had turned the world upside down.

The piece was extraordinary, as if Michelangelo's chisel was guided by the Lord Himself. I don't know how anyone could stand here and say that there is nothing divine about it. I wanted to reach through the glass and run my palm over the folds of Mary's skirt, down Christ's lean and muscled arm as it falls, lifeless, to the floor. The emotion embodied, that of a mother holding her child in death, stirred within me a profound sorrow.

I prayed for all mothers who had lost their children prematurely. I thought of my own son a world away and prayed that he was driving safely and making sound decisions. That he was healthy and alive. I thought of the thousands of women who've lost children on battlefields of one sort or another and never got that one final chance to cradle them, to anoint their hands and feet.

It was not until a bystander handed me a tissue that I realized I was weeping. "Thank you," I said to the elderly man in a black beret and a charcoal jacket buttoned to the collar.

"I come here many times," he said with a thick Italian accent, his eyes fixed on the sculpture. "Tears are common." I wiped my eyes and nodded. And we stood, elbow to elbow until he cleared his throat, blew his nose, and wandered out the door.

I continued slowly along the right side of the church to the Chapel of Saint Sebastian, honoring a martyr who was killed around AD 288, when he denounced the emperor for the persecutions of Christians. Beneath a mosaic of Sebastian's struggle lay the body of Pope

Innocent XI, known for his piety, preserved in a crystal casket for all the world to see. He was the first of three popes whose bodies were discovered to be incorrupt, the lack of decomposition a sign of holiness.

Further in, I happened upon the Blessed Sacrament Chapel, surrounded by an iron gate. A simple sign stood at its entrance: ONLY THOSE WHO WISH TO PRAY MAY ENTER. It is reserved for those who are not here just to tour, but who wish to sit in contemplation within the mystery that lies at the intersection of life and faith. Two large angels kneeling on either side of the altar beckoned me, but I was compelled to continue onward. I was not ready to sit with my thoughts.

I wandered to the middle of the center aisle and studied the ceiling with great intent. A shimmering gold frieze wrapped around the top of the nave. On it were Latin words with letters over six feet tall. It was a quote from the Gospel of Luke: "I have prayed for you, Peter, that your faith may never fail; and you in turn must strengthen your brothers."

I looked to my right at the papal altar, underneath which Saint Peter was buried. Luke's quote reminded me that Peter was just a man. I have always felt a sympathetic kinship with him. He was so very human, his foibles widely reported. He was, at times, uncouth, undiplomatic, and lacking tact. He fell asleep when he was supposed to be keeping watch. He faltered in faith and famously denied the one person he loved most. He was also brave, loyal, and tenacious. He knew when to ask for forgiveness, and he was willing to trust what he knew to be true in his heart, forging ahead to spread Christianity in a world that did not welcome him.

There are times when I have been sure of my faith, like Peter was the day he walked on the Sea of Tiberias toward Jesus, and times when I have questioned it wholeheartedly and sank, flailing in my own fear, like Peter did when he became afraid of the wind and began to sink.

Like him, too, I have continued to try. I continue to be pulled back to my center, back to the light. Have tried to strengthen my brothers and sisters in Christ. I love the notion of a great church built literally and figuratively upon a lowly fisherman, a regular guy. Don't we all start out that way? Don't we all begin in obscurity and ignorance and make our way toward enlightenment in fits and starts, one step forward and two steps back? Aren't we all called to the same journey of using our talents to lift and strengthen each other's faith?

There are sixteen statues that sit, reclining and relaxed, in flowing robes above the arches down both sides of the nave of the basilica. They represent the virtues calling us forward in our trek to the tabernacle. A visual reminder of the qualities we must seek and practice to lead a satisfying life. To become the best version of ourselves. As explained in Philippians 4:8, virtues are "whatever is true, whatever is honorable, whatever is just, whatever is pure, whatever is lovely, whatever is commendable."

Without warning, a rich deep baritone filled the air with song. Then a tenor voice started, and soon an entire choir joined in, creating an elegant harmony of chocolate notes, rich and decadent. The music, a Gregorian chant, pulled me forward. To the left side of the main altar, a grouping of chairs had been cordoned off. About a hundred people were seated, listening to the choir, and it dawned on me that it was Saturday night, and this was preparation for Mass. An usher granted me admission when I assured him that I was there to participate.

As I knelt and looked around, I saw people dressed in common clothes. It had never occurred to me that I could attend a service in this grand church. I hadn't realized that it was also a parish for those who lived nearby. Such is the danger of opulence, the thought that things are above us, that we are not deserving to be a part of such brilliance. The artists and architects of this basilica did their best to glorify God, but when all is said and done, this building would mean nothing without the interaction of human beings.

The voices of the choir soared, the timbre of angels. Rich and soulful, vaporous and mesmerizing, the music billowed around me. Taking a deep breath, the sweet, spicy tang of incense filled my lungs. I tilted my head back and opened my eyes. I studied the bronze canopy with its twisted columns spiraling into the dome hundreds of feet above. The notes of the chant drifted upward, whole notes and half notes caught in an updraft of longing, reflected in the glimmer of candlelight. I was suddenly dizzy, disoriented, and, for a brief enlightening moment, I couldn't decide if I was within this cathedral or if it was within me.

It is no wonder that we sense an indefinable weight as midlife approaches. We are carrying whole cathedrals within. As both artist and architect, we have each painstakingly and reverently constructed our life one block at a time from the moment of our birth. Now, fifty or so years hence, we are lined with side altars in tribute to those we have loved and those we have lost. We have hung paintings illustrating eras that have made us strong, and we are frescoed with depictions of those times we have been brought to our knees. Our memories flicker and illuminate, the voices of all we have known singing in the choir loft of our heart. Love is the incense that eddies and spirals around statues of parents, siblings, children, relatives, and treasured friends. Like the Duomo in Florence, we, at midlife, are great spiritual footprints upon the earth searching for a way to build the dome that will complete us.

I realized, while kneeling, why I have been, these past few years, inexplicably drawn to the sky, to the daytime blues, the brilliant sunsets, the stars, and the moon. Why I have been drawn to steps and climbing and searching. It is the fundamental act of looking upward that is instinctual. There are periods of seeking in our lives when we simply have to kneel down, look up, and listen. This was one of them.

By taking the time to journey, I was choosing to spend time in my own blessed chapel, that private place within where I could sit in contemplation of the mysteries that lie at the intersection of life and faith. I came to know, somehow, that God is within me and I am within Him.

I believe that the yearning—the emptiness, the restlessness—is all part of God's formula to catch our attention, drawing us inward to a place so quiet that we finally listen to his call. To that one true thing that makes our soul sing and our heartbeats match those of the universe. To the sort of life's work that makes sense in God's plan. To the work that will make our stained-glass windows glow with a fire from within and bring heaven's peace to our own little patch of earth. If we all felt the deep peace that such soul work brings, there would be little time for war, little reason for violence. It would be a world where every person could proudly say: *I am vast, I breathe grace, I hold within me God's proudest moments and greatest works.*

As I listened to Mass, in Italian, I could catch a word or phrase here and there, but most of the words were a blur, so I let the prayers and chants wrap themselves around me in a soft cocoon of holy sounds and sentimentality.

When Mass was over, I shuffled quietly around the altar. Night had fallen, and the candlelight was soft and ethereal. A womb. I didn't want to leave. An older gentleman with a kind face tapped on his wristwatch and steered me gently toward the exit.

With one last sweeping glance around the basilica, I exited down a hallway, past a gift shop. Outside, one of the Pope's Swiss guards stood in an archway in an orange-and-navy-striped uniform, a tall spear in his hand. Spotlights from all angles cut the piazza into triangles of light and shadow.

Deciding to skip the taxi, since it was a beautiful night, I walked down Via della Conciliazione and stopped for one final feast. I ate *gnocchi alla romana* (potato dumplings) and *saltimbocca alla romana* (veal scallops) at a delightful neighborhood *ristorante* where an attentive waiter went out of his way to make sure I didn't feel lonely. With a full stomach and a bursting heart, I collected my luggage at the train station and boarded the last train before midnight to the Hilton near the airport for a few hours of rest before my long journey home.

I was relaxed, filled with a sense of courage and excitement. I was ready to surrender wholly to whatever was *about to happen*. God had this midlife thing handled. I was finishing the era of child raising and ready for the assignment or adventure God would lay before me when He felt I was ready.

I had a strong feeling that it was time for me to, once again, put a pen to paper.

Texts from Home: Part 6

Me: Hi, Honey. Just checked in at Rome airport hotel. Beyond exhausted and looking forward to seeing my two favorite men.

Tim: Same here. Tired of chicken and Caesar salad. Talked to Katie. She sounds good.

Me: She'll be okay. She's ready.

Tim: Safe journey. House looks great but feels empty. Love you.

Me: Love you, too. So much. Text you from LAX.

Me: Matthew, see you soon!

Matthew: See you tomorrow night. We need groceries. Zucca has the big D again. Do you know where my extra basketball uniform is? Can I sleep over at Nick's house on Friday? Sorry if your car is out of gas. Xoxoxo

For I know the plans I have for you, declares the Lord, plans for welfare and not for evil, to give you a future and a hope. Then you will call upon me and come and pray to me, and I will hear you. *You will seek me and find me, when you seek me with all your heart.*
—Jeremiah 29: 11–13 (ESV)

NOTES

Notes:

"It's a Great Life if You Don't Weaken" was first published in *Tiferet Journal*, 2018.

"Seeking Adventure" was first published as "The Allure of Gray" in *The Sunlight Press*, 2018.

ACKNOWLEDGMENTS

First and foremost, I thank my husband, Tim, for his love and continued support. As most writers will attest, this craft is not an easy one, and, often, not a profitable one. It takes the support of family, friends, and colleagues to travel this road.

I thank my children, Katie and Matthew, for their love and support. I am endlessly proud of them, and they are my favorite human beings.

I thank my agent and friend, Judith Riven, for championing this manuscript. Her time and counsel have been a gift to me.

Finally, thank you, dear reader, for traveling with me and taking the time to ponder life's mysteries and challenges.